Quentin Tarantino

Another title in this series by the same author
Robert Crumb

Quentin Tarantino

D.K. Holm

www.pocketessentials.com

This edition published in December 2004 by Pocket Essentials
P.O. Box 394, Harpenden, Herts, AL5 1XJ
www.pocketessentials.com

Distributed in the USA by Trafalgar Square Publishing,
P.O. Box 257, Howe Hill Road, North Pomfret, Vermont 05053

A CIP catalogue record for this book is available from the British Library.

ISBN 1 904048 36 6

2 4 6 8 10 9 7 5 3 1

Typeset by Avocet, Typeset, Chilton, Aylesbury, Bucks
Printed and bound in Great Britain by Cox & Wyman, Reading

Acknowledgements

Anybody writing a book about Tarantino had better salute sources of inspiration and information or be himself charged with flagrant magpieism. To that end, I can begin with Chris Ryall, editor of Kevin Smith's web site, MoviePoopShoot.com, who has provided a welcoming virtual home for the past several years, and where many of this book's ideas were first developed. To him I can add Tim Appelo, Holly Cundiff, Manohla Dargis, Desiree French, Helaine Garren, Anne Hughes, Shawn Levy, Patti Lewis, Cynthia Lopez, Andrea Marsden, Cindy Mason, Gregg Morris, and Sam Smith, all making important contributions. Dawn Taylor provided crucial intel. Britta Gordon and Charles Schwenk provoked stimulating conversations. Especially resourceful were the rotating members of the Thursday night Aalto Lounge Round Table, including M. E. Russell, Robert Wederquist, Scott Anderson, Robert Lee, and the rest, including Damon Houx, our own personal Tarantino. Philip J. Brigham and several other readers of my movie column offered insights. I would also like to acknowledge the enthusiasm of Robert C. Cumbow, Karen Brooks, Rachel Byers, Manohla Dargis, Kim Morgan, Greg Reese, Scott Simmon and Audrey Van Buskirk. A large debt, literal and figurative, goes to Mary Catherine Lamb, who laboured long and hard on the manuscript, leaving only the errors I inserted later. In addition, Kristi Turnquist made numerous corrections and offered three interesting ideas, two of which I stole without acknowledgement. More generally, I can cite the Multnomah County Library, the Portland State University Library, and Powell's Books, plus the Internet Movie Database, both pro and civilian, which has been an essential resource, along with scores of web sites devoted to Tarantino. Acknowledgement is also due to publisher Ion Mills for his enthusiasm and risk-taking.

Contents

1. Introduction   9
*On writing a book about Tarantino; influences; the movie
industry before Tarantino; Tarantino's early life*

2. Dog Days   34
Reservoir Dogs (1992)

3. Pulp Fame   54
True Romance (1993), Natural Born Killers (1994)

4. Pulp Explosion   74
Pulp Fiction (1994)

5. Overexposure   93
*Hibernation; script polishing; acting; TV directing; talk
shows; The Man From Hollywood from Four Rooms
(1995); From Dusk Till Dawn (1996)*

6. The Wilderness Years   113
Jackie Brown (1997)

7. Pulp Exhaustion   125
Kill Bill, Vol. 1 (2003), Kill Bill, Vol. 2 (2004)

8. Geek World   139
Tarantinoesque; magpieism; the violence issue; future films;
Tarantino's status

9. Reference Materials   155

1. Introduction

WHY WRITING A BOOK ON TARANTINO IS THE HARDEST BOOK OF ALL

Writing about most film directors is easy.

Take David Cronenberg. Or Atom Egoyan. Or John Carpenter. Great filmmakers all – but when you confront the full spans of their careers, you don't really have to stray far from the films themselves, exceptions being the novels they are occasionally based on. There aren't a lot of pop references in their movies. Allusions to previous films and youth culture are minimal.

Cronenberg proudly proclaims (on the audio commentary track to the Blue Underground DVD of his 1979 race car film *Fast Company*) that unlike those of many of his peers, his films are based on books and his own life experiences rather than on other films. Egoyan's icy cogitations come partially from his ethnic background, indicating a high seriousness that aspires toward great art in the European tradition. With John Carpenter, once you've got Howard Hawks and *The Night Of The Living Dead*, you're in.

Quentin Tarantino, on the other hand, is an encyclopaedic artist. He draws on anything and everything at hand to tell his stories. He mirrors what in literature are called encyclopaedist authors, such as James Joyce, Thomas Pynchon, and William Gaddis.

I'm not saying that Tarantino is as 'great' as Joyce or Pynchon or Gaddis – but, then again, I'm not denying it (more on that later). As writers, Joyce and the others throw in everything they know, everything they remember reading, everything they've experienced. To fully understand and appreciate James Joyce, you have to be versed in British literature since *Beowulf* and the details of Irish history, in Catholicism, and in the topology of Dublin. Pynchon's *Gravity's Rainbow* demands familiarity with war-time London, the premises of behavioural psychology, aerial bombing technology, and African colonial history. Gaddis' *The Recognitions* requires a working knowledge of the American Puritan tradition, the techniques of art forgery, and Bohemian life in post-war Paris. And that's to name just a few topics for each of those writers who are immersed in the minutiae of everyday life, its newspapers, ditties, commercials, and lingo.

From the heights of Melville to the depths of Michener, this impulse to create a big, digressive book of life, an encyclopaedia containing all that the writer knows and feels is a fine (mostly American) literary tradition. The urge has passed on now to authors such as David Foster Wallace, William Vollmann and Dave Eggers. Tarantino, on the other hand, is a rarity: their cinematic equivalent. A typical Tarantino movie can cite '70s blaxploitation films, Japanese samurai films, or a Roy Rogers movie from the '40s. In a single 15-second section from *Kill Bill Vol. 2*, Tarantino manages to quote from an obscure movie called *Road To Salinas* and general car chase movies such as *Vanishing Point*, as well as from *Faster, Pussycat! Kill! Kill!*, *Dirty Mary Crazy Larry*, and *From Dusk Till Dawn* while also exploring, in almost essay-like form, the unexplored resonance of screen icons such as Daryl Hannah.

Indeed, if a film scholar finds enforced immersion in the real and cinematic world of Tarantino occasionally suffocating, he can always catch his breath by taking a side-trip to one of the several hundred films and filmmakers that inform Tarantino's work. Here are just some of the subjects it helps to be familiar with when viewing the films of Quentin Tarantino:

- Pulp fiction writers from the '20s and '30s, including Dashiell Hammett, Raymond Chandler, Raoul Whitfield, and Horace McCoy
- Crime writers from the '50s through the '70s, including Elmore Leonard and Charles Willeford
- Hong Kong action films from the '80s
- Blaxploitation films of the '70s
- The heist film genre
- Girl-gang movies
- Surf and hot rod music
- The '60s westerns of Monte Hellman
- Country-versus-city horror films such as *Deliverance*, *Two Thousand Maniacs*, and *I Spit On Your Grave*
- The work of Tony Scott, Brian De Palma, Abel Ferrara, Jean-Pierre Melville, and Howard Hawks
- '70s vigilante movies
- The films of Elvis Presley
- The couple-on-the-run genre
- The work of Oliver Stone
- Adult westerns of the '50s (Anthony Mann, Budd Boetticher, Robert Aldrich, Nicholas Ray, Samuel Fuller)
- The filmographies of favourite actors (Aldo Ray, Brian Keith, Charles Bronson, Sonny Chiba, and numerous others)
- '70s pop music
- Anything that might have been shown on television from 1966 to 1990

The only other contemporary filmmaker with a similar richness of reference, with an equal immersion in world cinema, is Canada's Guy Maddin (*Careful, The Saddest Music In The World*).

Still, as I hope this survey will show, Tarantino is more than just his references, those citations that so irritate writers who knock Tarantino for lack of invention, even though paradoxically it was the heavy references in *Kill Bill* that made audiences love him all over again. There are themes and images and obsessions peculiar to him. In addition to that, an audience with similar obsessions and backgrounds was ready for films from someone who shared their sensibility, which partially explains his sudden, intense popularity.

Here is an example of how downright obscure Tarantino's magpie art can get. I have a friend and colleague named Dawn Taylor. She is a movie reviewer for the *Portland Tribune* (www. portlandtribune.com) in Oregon. But she was raised in Southern California. She has a story about a particular Tarantino moment that she shared with me recently:

I grew up in Manhattan Beach, California, and for most of my life I lived in Los Angeles County's South Bay area, which mainly consists of the cities/suburbs of Manhattan Beach, Hermosa Beach, Redondo Beach, Torrance, Hawthorne, and Inglewood.

I'd moved to Portland, Oregon, from the L.A. area and was on a trip back down to Southern California to visit friends soon after Pulp Fiction *was released. My best friend, Mari Nolte, picked me up from the airport, and in the car I mentioned that we ought to go see this movie because it was directed by Quentin Tarantino, one of the guys who'd worked at our favourite, now-defunct local video store, Video Archives.*

We used to visit Video Archives fairly regularly, usually on our way to our weekly coffee marathon in a chain coffee shop called Coco's in the nearby shopping centre. It was the early days of video rentals, and there weren't a lot of places to go, and Video Archives had a really great selection – they also had an excellent shelf of 'staff picks' (go figure, given the staff) and they were always showing something interesting on an absolutely enormous TV in one corner. They had free popcorn, too.

Mari couldn't remember which one was Quentin Tarantino. 'Which one was he again?' she asked.

'The one named Quentin,' I said.

'Oh . . . the guy with the big head and the weird hair?'

'Yeah. That one.'

Mari, who still has her membership card, signed by Tarantino, had an account number that ended in 007, so every time Tarantino waited on her he made a James Bond joke.

We saw the movie at one of the local multiplexes and were, of course, blown away. One of the main talking points for us after the film was a bit of dialogue from the scene between Bruce Willis' Butch and Maria de Medeiros' Fabienne where she says she's going to go have breakfast, and she's going to have 'a big plate of blueberry pancakes with maple syrup, eggs over easy and five sausages . . . after that I'm going to have a slice of pie.' Butch says, 'Pie for breakfast?' and she replies, 'Any time of the day is a good time for pie.'

See, these weekly coffee get-togethers almost always involved eating pie (Coco's had great pie.) And because we always had pie, and because sometimes we'd only just recently had breakfast or lunch, or were planning on having breakfast but wanted pie too, one of our over-used in-jokes was to say to each other, 'Well, any time is a good time for pie.' We said this to each other frequently actually in Video Archives, in front of the staff.

So we're both convinced, to this day, that Tarantino overheard us in Video Archives and used our pie line in Pulp Fiction.

But more than being uniquely rife with cinematic quotes, the very texture of Tarantino's films goes against mainstream Hollywood's current aesthetic of surface blandness. His films are visually distinctive. His scripts juggle time and narrative order. His casting is seemingly eccentric but finely considered. Tarantino's movies demand careful attention because they were made with endless attention to detail. Tarantino shares this penchant with only a handful of other contemporary directors – including the Coen brothers, David Fincher, James Cameron, and Martin Scorsese – who walk in the footsteps of the scrupulous, patient Stanley Kubrick when it comes to attention to detail.

Tarantino breached the daunting boundaries of Hollywood, but unlike too many young Turks, he really likes movies. You'd think that Hollywood would welcome such dedicated film-making, but in fact it doesn't. Tarantino has made only five films in 12 years. This is partially due to a young man coping with the heady wine of success and who recoiled a bit after *Jackie Brown* from the demands made on him.

Given his spotty release rate and the critical contentiousness around him even among Hollywood power movers, it's convenient for Tarantino that he has a close artistic relationship with Miramax, which by all accounts supports the filmmaker to a degree matched only by its loyalty to Kevin Smith.

But imagine if Tarantino were at, say, Fox in the '90s during the last days of producer Art Linson's time there under Bill Mechanic, when Linson had Fincher making *Fight Club* (described in detail in Linson's book *What Just Happened?*). Or imagine Tarantino at Disney, or at DreamWorks, where he would most likely have been a hired hand, a *metteur en scene* instructed to move actors back and forth in front of a camera to achieve the required amount of footage per day. It's unlikely that Tarantino would have had the apparent freedom from meddling that he enjoyed otherwise. Hollywood isn't *inherently* evil, but in the balancing act of art, personal expression, and commerce, money usually dominates, if for no other reason than that you can't keep making movies unless they are making money. Tarantino would probably be moving around, as Peckinpah would say, like a whore, going where he's kicked, doing screenplays here, acting jobs there, and occasionally directing. He might be *just* what he does in his spare time – a script polisher on films such as *Crimson Tide.*

John Milius makes an evocative remark about Francis Ford Coppola in *Easy Riders, Raging Bull,* the documentary about '70s filmmakers based on Peter Biskind's controversial book. 'I thought that [Coppola] was just another mistake in the security of Hollywood,' Milius says. 'I looked at the whole thing as sort of a walled city, and there were breaches in the defences. Occasionally you could get in through one of these breaches and then see what was on the other side of the wall. That didn't mean that the police wouldn't find you sooner or later. He'd gotten on the wall somehow and gotten the local authorities convinced that he should be there. And of course he brought in the Trojan horse.'

It's a not uncommon attitude toward Hollywood. Actor Jeff Daniels is quoted in *The New Yorker* (19 August, 2004) saying of the Farrelly brothers that they are like 'lottery winners cut loose in Hollywood.' That's because they are Hollywood outsiders, men who cast their childhood friends in all their movies and are married to their pre-success sweethearts. They are Hollywood outsiders making hit Hollywood films. These days that's the profile of the best kinds of filmmakers. Tarantino is an outsider because, paradoxically, he loves movies and *wants to make good films*.

For Tarantino, you see, is a nerd. Or, more precisely, a film geek. And geeks – nerds – are not supposed to succeed in high-profile businesses such as movies (unless it's in a back-room occupation, such as the special effects department). Nerds aren't supposed to have ambition. Nerds are *supposed* to humbly accept their lot in life and toil at the service of the rich and beautiful. And nerds sure aren't supposed to be seen on the arms of the likes of Oscar winners such as Mira Sorvino and Sofia Coppola.

These assumptions about nerds, if you happen to share them, reveal a fundamental misunderstanding of them. You may have to be one to be able to explain it clearly or perceive the true reality of geekdom (this author can speak from experience), but surprisingly for the non-nerd, film geeks are just as competitive, aggressive, and ambitious as their athletic high-school tormentors. The field may be computers, statistics, video games, or movies, but geeks embrace their interests not just as complex hobbies that pass the time, but also as future career possibilities and life-or-death matters of importance.

A geek needs to be the smartest guy in the room. As collectors, geeks enjoy bragging rights. They like to say that they saw this or that movie first, or got advance tickets no one else had. They got the DVD early or for free. Or know someone who worked on it. And then this *same* geek will turn around and have really interesting ideas about the film.

Geeks tend to talk loud and laugh loud and in many other ways stick out in a crowd, thanks to their dress or manner or audio broadcast level, no matter how unintentionally. And though it's a horrible sight in many ways, a geek will not shrink from flirting with – or trying to pick up – a woman. A geek also has no shame about forcing himself on prestigious male strangers who might be able to advance his career. All in all, geeks resemble your average pushy Hollywood denizens, the Sammy Glicks of the town, but without the fashion sense and alterable interpersonal skills.

Geekdom, paradoxically, is part of Tarantino's appeal. Though there are undoubtedly people who have never heard of him or don't deem him important – retirees, insurance executives, and religious zealots – every geek knows his name. There is a lonely, lowly geek in some anonymous town who works in a video store or a Foot Locker, whose weekends are filled with marathon movie watching and whose diet consists of hamburgers and pizzas and who's always nursing that screenplay that never gets beyond page 60. This geek looks up to Tarantino. This director gives that fanboy hope. Tarantino's very success suggests that other lowly geeks can breach the walls of the industry and get their visions committed to film.

What distinguishes Tarantino from these powerless geeks? It's hard to say, but surely it is no *one* thing. Tarantino had an ambitious, competent, successful, and well-educated mother who (eventually, anyway) served as a role model for him. Equally important, Tarantino is hyper-conscious of his career trajectory. Not only has he studied movies and movie directors, he has studied movie directors' careers, their ups and downs, their rhythms, the consequences of choices, and the quality of public perceptions. One famous anecdote from Tarantino's early years is about his interviewing several directors, including Milius and Joe Dante (and possibly Walter Hill and Brian De Palma, although the complete list of interview subjects is not known), on the pretext that he was writing a Bogdanovich-style book, interviews during which he reportedly asked these masters probing questions about career management. It is to be hoped that whatever he heard from them kept Tarantino in good stead during that rough phase of his own career when he went from critical darling to pariah.

I can attest to this critical fluctuation because I myself fell victim to it. Or perhaps I should rephrase it and say that I, too, was a Tarantino victimizer, if only in a modest unrecognised way, writing for an obscure, now defunct, but once much-loved newspaper called *PDXS* in Portland, Oregon.

I first heard of Tarantino from a small notice by (I believe) Donald Lyons in a 1992 issue of *Film Comment*, noting that a film called *Reservoir Dogs* was the hot movie out of Sundance that year, that this film (as had the earlier *One False Move*) took crime thrillers in a new and refreshing direction. A student of *noir*, I became instantly excited. This enthusiasm for an unseen film was realized several months later, when as a movie reviewer I saw an advance screening at a cinema called the

KOIN Centre Cinemas in downtown Portland. It more than lived up to its hype.

Then, when Tarantino suddenly had two in-production screenplays in the theatrical pipeline (*True Romance, Natural Born Killers*), I realized that he had gone in the opposite of the expected direction, establishing himself first as a director before the two other films from his scripts appeared (which would have established him as, say, another Shane Black, the screenwriter famously paid millions for his scripts). Later I realized that this was another example of Tarantino's cunning career-management technique. When *Pulp Fiction* arrived, I loved that film, too.

But then came Tarantino's various acting endeavours for other directors (*Destiny Turns On The Radio*, et al.), and his high-profile television appearances; and then after reading three mostly cutting biographies of him published nearly simultaneously, I began to sour on Tarantino, as many did. Most damning in that 'disillusionment' was the intellectual property theft that became such a prominent part of his career gestalt. For me, much of *Pulp Fiction* was subsequently tarnished by the realization that so many others contributed to the script in ways small and large. Probably the worst account of Tarantino was *Killer Instinct*, the story of the making of *Natural Born Killers* by Jane Hamsher, who co-produced it, which made Tarantino seem like a near-literate careerist turncoat fraud.

What was telling, and which I didn't realize fully at the time, was that I was still reading about him. He proved to be a director you always wanted to learn more about. As more books and articles and talk-show appearances accumulated, I gobbled them up, insatiable for more about the person I no longer (ostensibly) respected.

Then with the release of *Jackie Brown*, the 'rehabilitation' began. It was conventional for people to say that it's his best film, and the critical consensus appeared to be that this was a new, 'mature' Tarantino who had put aside his childish toys to dwell Peckinpah-ishly on mature characters gazing into the light of dusk.

Then there was a long absence. What was Tarantino doing? As the years between *Jackie Brown* added up – two years, three years, six years – I suddenly found myself *missing* Tarantino. There is no way to prove this, but I believe that a lot of the goodwill bestowed on *Kill Bill* was borne from just downright missing the guy and his movies.

That was because Tarantino had spoken to a new kind of filmgoer – and most of them remained loyal, despite protests to the contrary. There was an audience for his movies back in 1992, and Tarantino appeased it. He not only filled a cinematic need, but he created new viewers for his work. The audience was ready for Tarantino, and he was ready for them, and together they created a new film genre.

By 1994, a new descriptive critical term appeared: 'Tarantinoesque.' Like 'Kafkaesque' before it (or 'Wellesian,' or 'Hitchcockian'), it seemed to say everything and nothing at the same time. Or perhaps it should be put this way: The reader knew what was meant without necessarily being able to define the term.

It was a new genre. Let's use the portmanteau phrase *film voir* to label this odd, characteristically '90s genre, taking the phrase film noir and substituting one of the syllables from *reservoir*. A *film voir* is a crime film with a comic bent tending to juggle the time frame or narrative order, with side helpings of pop-culture references delivered in lengthy Godardian conversations and monologues and cast with a blend of achingly hip youngsters and ageing cult figures, and then sweetened with vivid if not necessarily excessive violence. Typical examples of *film voir* might be *The Usual Suspects* and *8 Heads In A Duffle Bag*. It's a remarkable achievement. Tarantino has created something distinct and original by ransacking the whole history of cinema.

D.K. HOLM

Influences On Tarantino

A catalogue of Tarantino influences could be extensive and exhausting if the writer got carried away. But a basic core list of filmmakers exists without whom Tarantino is unimaginable – or enjoyable.

Brian De Palma (1940–): Probably Tarantino's favourite director, the acolyte borrows De Palma's use of the split screen, his approach to music, and in a modest way his theme of betrayal between friends. The son of a surgeon (and so, he says, inured to the image of blood), the Newark, New Jersey-born director made several truly independent comic features in the '60s, contemporaneously with his oft-times polar opposite, John Cassavetes. De Palma began to gather cult attention with horror films such as *Sisters* (1973) and then *Carrie* (1976), made in a genre he mined for several years. Hit films include *Scarface* (1983), *The Untouchables* (1987), and *Mission: Impossible* (1996). Tarantino frequently mentions *Blow Out* (1981) as his all-time favourite movie, and he also holds *Casualties Of War* (1989) in high esteem. Tarantino took acting lessons from Allen Garfield (née Goorwitz) partially because Garfield had worked on De Palma's early films.

Howard Hawks (1886–1977): One of the primary masters of the art of American cinema, Hawks (born to a wealthy family in Goshen, Indiana) worked in a wide variety of genres, such as the gangster film (*Scarface*, 1932), westerns (*Red River*, 1948), science fiction (*The Thing From Another World*, 1951, which, officially, Hawks produced), the race car movie (*The Crowd Roars*, 1932, and *Red Line 7000*, 1965), and others, yet maintained a remarkable consistency among all his films, even using the same bits of dialogue decades apart. Hawks' movies are about men on a mission, prizing competence and conviviality above all traits, and his narratives often alternate between the men on the road or engaging in their tasks with scenes of them back at the clubhouse or around a campfire, when the lessons in manliness learned in the field are quietly enacted in private. Tarantino has said in interviews that he uses *Rio Bravo* (1959) as a litmus test for potential girl-friends.

Stanley Kubrick (1928–1999): Besides the obvious parallels between *The Killing* (1956) and *Reservoir Dogs*, Kubrick provides two specific hallmarks for Tarantino to follow. The first is attention to detail, waiting patiently to get it right (Kubrick was capable of waiting decades to get it right). The second is the importance of casting. Trained as an actor first, Tarantino (like Paul Thomas Anderson) is sympathetic to actors and directs them well. But the biggest hurdle is getting the right people in the first place. Kubrick was capable of getting unnervingly great performances from the most unlikely people because he knew that they fitted into his overall vision and the context of the film. Cunningly or not, Tarantino has inherited an eye for perfect casting.

Sergio Leone (1929–1989): If the great director of spaghetti westerns contributed anything to the generations that followed him, it was the confidence to enact his rituals slowly, and alternating provocatively between close-ups and beautiful panoramas, sometimes in the same shot. In his three westerns with Clint Eastwood, and in *Once Upon A Time In The West* (1969), Leone created a world of masculine codes of violence in a world in which life is cheap. Leone brazenly innovated by often showing women and children slaughtered by his nefarious gunmen and by lavishly saturating his desert settings with blood.

Jean-Pierre Melville (1917–1973): Among the most admirable aspects of this French director's films for our purposes is his obsession with the rituals and codes of criminals and the paradoxes of luck. *Bob Le Flambeur (Bob The Gambler,* 1955) puts forward a very clever narrative trick for a punch line, while *Le Samouraï* (1967) is the *ne plus ultra* of moody gangster films in which stoic courage under fire masks a bleak romanticism. There is something beautiful in the way Melville takes so seriously what to others would be a childish or inconsequential game. Melville, like his disciple, is a connoisseur of the futile gesture and the passing moment. *Le Cercle Rouge* (*The Red Circle*, 1970) is just plain crazy and complex. Tarantino says that *Le Doulos* (*The Finger Man*, 1963) is one of his all-time favourite films. The trail from Melville to Woò to Tarantino is a kind of aesthetic game of Chinese whispers.

Jean-Luc Godard (1930–): A 'founding father' of the French New Wave in the years after filmmakers such as Melville and Jacques Becker showed a new way to make movies, Godard, who balances politics and aesthetics in his work (his films often seem more like essays on cinema than actual movies), I would guess that Godard's early films (*A Woman Is A Woman*, 1961; *Contempt*, 1963; and *Bande A Part*, 1964 after which Tarantino named his production company) had the most impact on Tarantino, with their romanticism, their love of being in love, their distanced scrutiny of 'Woman', their cartoon-like gangsterism, and their long signature conversation sequences, in which lovers talk at length (20 minutes of screen time is an average) in their apartments. The long hand-held take on Bruce Willis in *Pulp Fiction* is a good example.

Abel Ferrara (1951–): A native New Yorker who directed some of the most controversial films of the early '80s (*The Driller Killer, 1979; Ms. 45*, 1981), Ferrara is the poet of fiercely masculine men on the edge of madness. Though the ambiguous *Bad Lieutenant* (1992) is arguably his most successful and most critically acclaimed film, other movies, such as *King Of New York* (1990) and the later *The Funeral* (1996), unveil the qualities that Tarantino most likely admires, a stripped-down and intense macho milieu in which self-absorption alternates with a kind of ritualistic violence. Both Ferrara and Tarantino prove to be among the few directors to use Harvey Keitel to his best advantage.

The State Of The Movie Industry When Tarantino Emerged

By the time that Quentin Tarantino came on the cinematic scene, the country and the film industry had emerged from the '80s of Ronald Reagan. To some outside observers, the movies had been given over to filmmakers doing high-budget versions of the serials and B movies of their youth (*The Empire Strikes Back*, *E.T.: The Extra-Terrestrial*, *Ghostbusters*, *Batman*). Though there was a dark mirror industry of political films during that period (*Salvador*, *Under Fire*), *Top Gun* is probably the signature film of the era – jingoistic, flashy, and stereotypical on the surface while homoerotic and narratively incoherent on a deeper level. (Tarantino has a complex, amusing, and interesting relationship with that film, and its director, Tony Scott, which we'll get into later.)

But the Hollywood industry was also changing throughout that time, creating a Petri dish in which Tarantino's talent could find purchase. The rising so-called independent film movement, which would later for all intents and purposes be co-opted by the major studios for its own purposes, was creating opportunities for young filmmakers that were unheard of since the early '70s, with brief oases of opportunity at particular moments in the '50s and '60s. Having its immediate roots as far back as 1977, the indie movement was encouraged by, among other things, the Sundance Film Festival and related workshops and the sudden rise of numerous small distributors, almost all of which that didn't simply fold, later incorporated into the majors. The banner year of the indies was probably 1986, which saw the release of some 22 films considered to be independent by one criterion or another (*Blue Velvet, Desert Hearts, Down By Law, Heavy, Parting Glances,* and *She's Gotta Have It* among them).

What this means, of course, is that seed money was available for filmmakers making the leap from short films to features, or from provocative screenplays to directing (Tarantino's route). As the 1990s began, so-called independent film was a strong force in the industry, and companies such as Miramax, New Line, and Live Entertainment took over with their art films and horror hits from fading companies such as exploitation specialist Cannon or Sir Lew Grade. This was the setting into which Tarantino appeared to emerge so suddenly in 1992.

Tarantino's Early Life

Many aspects of Tarantino's life are well known – four formal biographies of him have already been published. And Tarantino is not above a bit of self-mythologizing for dramatic effect, like most film directors – after all, movies are a theatrical art form. Thus certain components of Tarantino's life story have solidified into received truth: the Cherokee heritage, the hillbilly background, the saga of the struggling but self-determined single mother, the problems at school, the events surrounding his first film, and the video-store-clerk-to-film-director Cinderella story.

These elements of his life make up The Mythology, the parallel, media-based life story next to the real one that Tarantino has actually lived. For the most part we don't know and will never know the second. The movie-going public can only know The Mythology. And many parts of The Mythology may very well be true. We have to take it on trust that the four bios and the scores of magazine profiles have in at least some ways not just circled the truth but actually captured it. But what is certainly true is that many aspects of Tarantino's life are what Norman Mailer, in his first book on Marilyn Monroe, called factoids: untruths or urban legends that have been willed into being by repetition in the mass media. Separating the facts from the factoids in a small general guide to Tarantino is impossible, but at least the broad narrative elements are widely agreed upon.

Quentin Tarantino was born on 27 March, 1963, in Knoxville, Tennessee. His mother was the former Connie McHugh. He was named after Quint Asper, the character Burt Reynolds played in the CBS western series *Gunsmoke* from 1962 to 1965, as well as after characters in Faulkner's *The Sound And The Fury*. His mother, only 16 at Tarantino's birth, was born in Tennessee but raised around Ohio and the Midwest with relatives. During a brief sojourn in Los Angeles, she met and married a law student and aspiring actor named Tony Tarantino. The marriage, seemingly committed to in order to gain emancipation from her parents, did not last long, and the woman now named Connie Tarantino moved back to her mother's in Knoxville. There she learned, to her surprise, that she was pregnant. A strong-willed, independent woman, Tarantino's mother decided to have the unexpected child out of wedlock while pursuing a medical degree.

It's unclear whether Tarantino has ever met his father, but the senior Tarantino does have a web site (www.tonytarantino.com), where he takes pride in his son's achievements.

In 1966, after having completed her nursing course, Connie Tarantino moved back to Los Angeles (ostensibly for the weather), settling in the South Bay area of southern Los Angeles. Young Tarantino was to spend most of his youth there.

During this time, Connie made a switch from medical practice to administration, eventually becoming a market-ing executive in the California branch of a Maryland-based HMO, or Health Maintenance Organisation, a form of group health insurance that offers members the services of various participating institutions and physicians. In Los Angeles, she met and married musician Curtis Zastoupil. He became the first of what would become several father figures to young Quentin (Connie Zastoupil has been married three times).

As a kid, Tarantino showed a typical interest in comic books and movies and a lack of interest in school, especially Hawthorne Christian School, the Catholic day school he attended around age nine, where uniforms were required. His one friend around this time was a neighbour named Kevin Minky. Part of Tarantino lore is that his mother did not pre-censor the movies she took him to and that *Carnal Knowledge* (1971) and *Deliverance* (1972) were early films mother-and-son saw together. As Connie Zastoupil's career took off, Curtis Zastoupil became a regular movie-going companion for Quentin, until the Zastoupils divorced around 1973 (at which point his mother sent Tarantino to live with his grandparents in Tennessee for somewhere between six months and a year, a move undertaken because she had been diagnosed with Hodgkin's disease, though it proved to be a misdiagnosis). She later married Jan Bohusch, a trade show promoter, in a union that lasted for eight years. Young Tarantino and Bohusch were both movie mad and saw many films together. The family lived in a split-level home in the Palo Del Amo Woods section of Torrance, though Tarantino liked to see movies in the rough areas of South Bay, such as the Carson Twin Cinemas.

His mother has noted the ongoing creativity he demon-strated in various Mother's Day stories he wrote for her, and at 14 he wrote a screenplay called *Captain Peachfuzz And The Anchovy Bandit*, derived from the Burt Reynolds car chase film *Smokey And The Bandit*, in which the bandit of the title steals pies from pizza parlours. At 15, he was arrested for shoplifting a copy of Elmore Leonard's *The Switch* from a Kmart, a weird blend of literariness and criminal opportunism with an inter-esting aftermath (see the *Jackie Brown* chapter). Grounded for the summer, Tarantino emerged only to join the Torrance Community Theatre, where he acted in the plays *Two Plus Two Makes Sex* and *Romeo And Juliet*.

Tarantino dropped out of school at 16. His mother describes her son as having a genius-level IQ, but he was also saddled with poor spelling habits and an inability to tell time, add up, or perceive geographical directions. Lying about his age, Tarantino got a job as an usher in an adult venue, the Pussycat Theatre in Torrance, where he tore tickets, among other conventional duties. (According to one report, he was fired after an angry friend snitched to management about his real age.) At this time he also started using the name Tarantino (though legally it may still be Zastoupil).

Let's assess what we've established so far: a lonely kid with few if any friends but with a close and supportive family. He also has an ego fuelled by his mother's attentions and 'tough love.' Yet at the same time the prideful youth is not above arguing with her, even while he is learning from her the tenacity that helped create his success while other geeks failed. She is a model for ambition and success. He grows up perhaps not really understanding friendship or loyalty even though they fascinate him and become themes of his future films.

In his late teens, Tarantino was apparently estranged from his mother, but the now-aspiring actor enrolled in acting classes at the James Best Theatre Company (Best played a character on the comic car chase TV series *The Dukes Of Hazzard*). The classes were taught mostly by Jack Lucarelli. In 1983, just turned 20, Tarantino moved out of his mother's house entirely (in December 1981 Connie remarried, but that union was not a happy one, though Tarantino occasionally did work for his new step-father). In 1984 he began working on the script of an eventually abandoned film called *My Best Friend's Birthday*, conceived by Craig Hamann, whom he met in James Best's acting class. Other students in the class, some of whom turn up in Tarantino's films, were Rich Turner, Rick Squery, Brenda Hillhouse, and Brenda Peters. Tarantino and Hamann often wrote their own scenes instead of drawing upon theatrical literature. Hamann also introduced Tarantino to Cathryn Jaymes, who was to be Tarantino's manager for the next ten years (and as so often happens in his life, Tarantino met her on his birthday). During this time, Tarantino managed to get one known professional acting job, as an Elvis impersonator in an episode of the fourth season of *The Golden Girls* called *Sophia's Wedding: Part 1* which aired on 19 November 1988. He also managed to get a job as, of all things, a head-hunter for the aerospace industry, which allowed him to move into a nicer apartment on Elderglen Lane in Harbor City (near the airport) and buy a Honda Civic. Significant movies he saw around this time were *Blowout,* the Richard Gere remake of *Breathless,* and *The Border.*

That same year he began what turned out to be a five-year-stint working in a shop called Video Archives and during which time he developed a competitive relationship with co-worker Roger Avary. He also met a handful of other film geeks there who would later influence his movies and with whom he would have often-contentious relations (according to The Mythology, one co-worker, Scott McGill, committed suicide because he feared that he wouldn't have as successful a career as Tarantino or Avary). In 1983 Tarantino came up with the scheme of writing (or pretending to write) a book of inter-views with film directors, in the manner of Peter Bogdanovich. In 1985, now 22, Tarantino started taking acting lessons from a sympathetic Allen Garfield. Tarantino had sought out Garfield because he had worked with De Palma, though the actor surprised the acolyte by being critical of the cinematic god. Tarantino also met John Langley, the eventual producer of the TV show *Cops,* who hired him to do grunt work on a Dolph Lundgren exercise infomercial *Dolph*

Lundgren: Maximum Potential. Another project with Hamann that Tarantino had going around this time was a screenplay called *Criminal Mind*, about a serial killer who quits, baffling investigators. The Mythology reports a few incidents of violence taking place in Video Archives when customers pushed Tarantino too far, and the reader of these accounts wonders how the store could have borne up legally and financially as a result of these incidents if they indeed happened.

Somewhere in this time frame, Tarantino and co-worker McGill (the son of the man who previously owned Video Archives) began work on a short film called *Lovebirds In Bondage.* The plot concerns a guy who has himself committed to an asylum so that he can be near his girlfriend, who's been traumatized by a car accident. Only footage of Tarantino (as the lover) ended up being shot, and then the film was mysteriously or ambiguously destroyed. McGill was a close friend of Avary's and worked on one of his short films as well.

Tarantino and Hamann, along with other collaborators, including Rand Vossler, finally started shooting *My Best Friend's Birthday* in 1986, borrowing cameras, and using their friends and family's homes as sets. Tarantino also convinced Garfield to play a small part. The production went awry, however. A camera, borrowed from Cormanesque producer Charles Band, didn't synch sound correctly. Then, after a series of frustrations, some of the footage was destroyed at a processing lab. Tarantino finally gave up on it.

The surviving footage apparently enjoys split ownership between Tarantino and Hamann, but about an hour's worth is available on DVD. Not incompetently shot (in black and white) and edited, the footage's primary interest comes from showing the inchoate Tarantino exploring the art form. Much of the plot of *Birthday* (as far as can be deduced from the fragments) was later recycled into *True Romance.* There is even a cocaine overdose that anticipates *Pulp Fiction*'s heroin OD.

Characters have movie posters on the wall whether they make sense to the scene or not. Tarantino's acting skills have not necessarily altered over the years, but a long sequence of post-intimacy chat with the hooker his character bought for his best friend (in which Tarantino's character confesses that he has a foot fetish) shows the influence of Godard and his long scenes between couples in apartments. It is interesting to note that Tarantino casts himself not as the loser main character – as most self-pitying nerds might – but as the roué.

After this, the truly productive years began. Tarantino started writing *True Romance* in 1987, and then the next year, at the age of 26, he wrote *Natural Born Killers* (*NBK*) and *Reservoir Dogs* (its progenitor, Ringo Lam's *City On Fire,* was released in 1987). In 1989, Tarantino met Grace Lovelace, an education student who later went on to become an academic, and got her a job at Archives. Before dating her, Tarantino himself quit Video Archives in 1989, ending up the next year at a company called Imperial, which also dealt in videos. This was the year that Tarantino was arrested for outstanding parking fines. One biographer has him in the slammer conceiving the idea for *NBK.*

Eventually, Tarantino made a contact at another company, CineTel. Representatives met with him and others involved with *True Romance* in summer 1991. They liked his earlier scripts, and Catalaine Knell hired him to do a significant rewrite on a straight-to-video movie called *Past Midnight*, his first screen credit (though as associate producer).

Only partially written by Tarantino, and done so within a production history that makes it difficult to officially segregate Tarantino's contributions from that of the credited scripter, Frank Norwood (the last of that writer's official credits), *Past Midnight* (1992) nevertheless contains some elements, present in a ghostly fashion, that announce or anticipate Tarantino's cinematic personality. Director Jan Eliasberg, however, didn't like some of his ideas, such as the insertion of an unwanted foot massage (which becomes the offer of a backrub) and a mentally retarded character.

Past Midnight (the title means nothing in the context of the movie) is linked by its few reviewers (and even its writer) to *Jagged Edge* (1985), though that comparison is a little misleading. In reality *Past Midnight* is one of several thousand lugubrious and remarkably similar straight-to-video 'erotic thrillers,' usually revolving around a terrorized woman. In this one she is Laura Mathews (Natasha Richardson, looking a bit like Liza Minnelli). She is a social worker handed the case of one Ben Jordan (Rutger Hauer), just out of prison for killing his pregnant wife some 17 years earlier. Mathews, who has a platonic friendship with office mate Steve Lundy (a slightly miscast Clancy Brown) has just returned from the funeral of her beloved father and now finds herself falling for the irascible and troubled Jordan, whom she comes to believe is innocent, thanks to some amateur detective investigations on the side. Tarantino has told interviewers that the scenes between Clancy and Richardson bear his hand, but those between Richardson and Hauer do not. Yet we first encounter moments that are now called Tarantinoesque in Mathews and Jordan's first scene together, in which they compare the mysteries of David Goodis and John D. MacDonald, as well as in a shot (done earlier in the film) of an old Dell mystery cover found in a trunk of Mathews' dad's effects.

Past Midnight bears some of the tedious markings of these low-budget, straight-to-video features: a paucity of sets, none of which looks lived in, a leaden pace and a ponderous editing style that treats all scenes as being of equal weight. But the film is not without its modest flourishes, such as the windshield wiper that slashes like a knife across the pane of Mathews' window of her Scout International while she is sitting next to the ominous Jordan, or the foreboding crows reflected in the skylight through which we see Mathews and Jordan make love for the first time. *Past Midnight's* opening scene is faintly reminiscent of *Halloween* (a shattered figure exiting a house at night with a bloody knife). But aside from these daring influences, director Eliasberg (who later went on to direct *Dawson's Creek,* among numerous other examples of series television) does a weak job of first convincing us that Hauer is the killer, and than later that he isn't. On the other hand, she handles well an interesting self-conscious movie angle to the story: the serial killer films his murders and they figure in the plot, with Mathews viewing the old footage seized at the crime scene as well as watching new footage left in her house. After she puts one small Super 8 reel into her projector, the first image Mathews sees is the wall itself that she uses as a screen; then the camera pans to the right to the short staircase that leads to her upstairs bed and bath. This unnerving movie-within-a-movie doubling is like something that De Palma might do (certainly going over and over the same footage resembles De Palma in *Blow Out* and its inspiration, Antonioni's *Blowup*) and may well have come from the pen of Tarantino. But it also weirdly anticipates the Robert Richardson-inspired film stock mélange of Oliver Stone's version of *Natural Born Killers.*

Thematically, *Past Midnight* also harbours an interesting nexus of psychological crosshatchings concerning mothers and fathers that doesn't really bear much on Tarantino's later films – but does mirror interestingly some of his biographical experience. Mothers have been a trope in serial-killer thrillers since *Psycho* and fathers since *Peeping Tom.* The script to *Past Midnight* mixes them all together with father substitutes and weird incest allusions. Mathews is more or less in love with her father, while the serial killer was the actual, if forced, lover of his own mother (thus the psychological explanation for his slaying of pregnant women). There is a hint that the killer's brother (Paul Giamatti in an early role) is also his son (a la

Chinatown?). Meanwhile Jordan is something of a father figure to Mathews, even though from narrative clues the viewer knows that Lundy is actually more like her father. All this is tangled up with the biographical details of Tarantino's life, the abandoning father, the subsequent father figures and mentors, the weird blend of competition with and inspiration from his own youngish mother.

Around the same time Tarantino was paid to turn a treatment by special effects wizard Robert Kurtzman, of KNB EFX Group, into the script *From Dusk Till Dawn*. It's not clear how Kurtzman heard of Tarantino – he may have been one of many recipients of Tarantino screenplays from his manager at the time – but he hired the aspiring writer and actor to convert the treatment into an 80-page script that Kurtzman would use as the basis for his own directorial debut. Tarantino is also said to have done a script rewrite for the partners Ron Hamady and George Braunstein for a film about a man who seeks revenge on the pirates who killed his wife and son on their 60-foot yacht. Apparently the script was never filmed. Shortly thereafter he got into the Sundance screenwriting workshops with *Reservoir Dogs,* in June of 1991 (but also broke up with Lovelace at the same time); he shot the film from late summer to autumn of 1991. The film made the festival rounds in early 1992 (it made its debut at Sundance in January) and was released by Live Entertainment in the autumn of 1992. Neither the world nor Tarantino have been the same since. After years of frustration, Tarantino's career had finally started . . .

2. Dog Days

'Overnight success' is an acridly inaccurate phrase, especially when it comes to the career of Quentin Tarantino, a man who had been dreaming about, rehearsing for, and trying to get into the movies since he was a teen. What to the public is the sudden revelation of an assured artist coming out of left field is to the artist very possibly the achingly long-delayed fruit falling from a very bitter tree.

By the age of 27, Tarantino was fairly discouraged. He had spent most of the 1980s trying to make movies but hadn't advanced at all far.

Still, he was ever so close to the brink of success. By 1990 he had sold one screenplay *(From Dusk Till Dawn)*, had written two more that were read by numerous people in town, and had been paid to do a page one rewrite on an erotic thriller.

But once Tarantino decided to write a heist film and make that his directorial debut, inspired in part by all the heist films he had viewed while at Video Archives, the magic began. Originally he was going to collaborate with Roger Avary on an anthology film of crime stories, with different parts to be directed by different friends, and what became *Reservoir Dogs* is said to have been just one of those stories.

In 1989, Tarantino was living in a cheap apartment on the corner of Western and Third in Hollywood. He was working at Imperial Entertainment, a small production/distribution company. Tarantino made cold calls to video shops to promote

Imperial's VHS tapes. Editing a movie in the same building was one Sheldon Lettice, who worked on various Jean-Claude Van Damme movies. Through Lettice Tarantino met Scott Spiegel, a friend of Sam Raimi. Tarantino proved to be not only one of the few people to have seen Spiegel's debut, *Intruder* (1988), a low-budget horror film set in a shopping mall, but could actually quote its dialogue. Spiegel had co-written a Clint Eastwood movie that was about to come out, *The Rookie*, and went on to become one of two or three unsung heroes behind Tarantino's success. They became friends and shared an interest in the comedian Rudy Ray Moore, who had been in numerous blaxploitation films and who served as an influence on Tarantino. Moore did bits that were sometimes given in a sing-song de Livery that some believe was the first manifestation of rap.

Spiegel and Tarantino were queuing to watch *House Of Wax* and a Three Stooges movie when Tarantino was introduced to Spiegel's friend Lawrence Bender, a former dancer turned actor who had produced *Intruder*. Nothing momentous happened on that occasion, but later at a Memorial Day barbecue at Spiegel's place, Tarantino fell into a chat with Bender. Apparently Bender had read *True Romance* in his capacity as a producer, and they also touched upon *Natural Born Killers* and Tarantino's idea for *Reservoir Dogs*, though he had not yet written it. Tarantino's description of it as a heist film in which you don't see the heist intrigued Bender. Among Bender's bits of advice was that Tarantino actually write the script.

When he returned to the Imperial offices, Tarantino hauled out *Intruder* and watched it numerous times to study Bender's producing techniques. (*Reservoir Dogs* is said by some to mimic *Intruder*.) Then, in June, Tarantino wrote the script over the course of three intense weeks. When he finished, he called a surprised Bender. The script was apparently not in what you would call a traditional format, but Bender found himself excited about it anyway and wanted to buy an option. But Tarantino wanted to make a film before his 28th birthday, and that was a mere six months away. Tarantino, tired of producers taking too long to get something going, allowed Bender only a two-month option, after which, he said, Tarantino would shoot the film himself, using the sum he got from the sale of *True Romance* ($30,000). As perhaps a form of consolation, Tarantino said that they would film it quickly in black and white, with Tarantino as Mr. Pink and Bender playing Nice Guy Eddie.

Finally, fed up with his crummy neighbourhood in Hollywood, Tarantino moved to his mother's house in Glendale in late summer 1990, his faraway exile and car-lessness about to create a series of problems for him. Among the projects he worked on was a novel about his Video Archives years, patterned after Larry McMurtry's novel *All My Friends Will Be Strangers*. He finished only two chapters, but if he ever completes it or turns it into a script, the result could be his, and his generation's, own *American Graffiti*.

Bender hit the phones and tried to drum up some money. One potential Canadian investor, so goes The Mythology, said he would produce it if his girlfriend could play Mr. Blonde. At the same time Bender was attending acting classes, taught by Peter Floor. Bender told Floor about *Reservoir Dogs*. Floor asked Bender who, of all actors, he envisioned in the film. Bender replied, Harvey Keitel. Floor replied that his ex-wife, Manhattan acting coach Lilly Parker, knew Keitel from the Actor's Studio. Floor sent the script to Parker, who gave it to Keitel. He called Bender on a Sunday, the morning after he read the script, saying he wanted to do it. Keitel became *Reservoir Dogs'* father figure, helpful but also at times firm.

Meanwhile, Bender's roommate had a friend named Lori (or sometimes Laurie) who knew Monte Hellman, another one of Tarantino's many heroes. Over the phone, the friend read bits of the script to Hellman, who demanded the chance to read the whole piece immediately.

According to The Mythology, Hellman was excited by *Reservoir Dogs* and wanted to direct it. But the text was a mess. Hellman took the manuscript pages, formatted the script, and cleaned it all up. Hellman met Bender and then met Tarantino at the now-defunct C. C. Brown's on Hollywood Boulevard, where Tarantino convinced Hellman that the writer should also be the director. (Tarantino had just received the money for *True Romance* and felt he could do it himself, guerrilla-style.) Still wanting to participate, Hellman ended up becoming equal partners with Tarantino and Bender. Hellman may have mortgaged his house along with some land in Texas to finance production (bios are inconsistent on this point). He was able to turn up a number of funding possibilities, but ultimately those potential investors demanded too many compromises of Tarantino's vision.

Hellman knew Richard Gladstein of Live Entertainment (now Artisan, recently absorbed by Lion's Gate), which was then the video arm of Carolco, Live being a straight-to-video movie production and distribution company. (For Live, Hellman and Gladstein had done a sequel to *Silent Night, Deadly Night* together.)

On 4 February 1991, Gladstein met with the crew and came up with a list of potential cast members who would make the film worth Live's risk: Dennis Hopper, Christopher Walken (who could have been Mr. Orange), and Keitel. Keitel apparently had tried to interest Walken and Hopper, but they couldn't make a commitment (though later they were both to become closely identified with Tarantino's films). Nevertheless, in April, papers were signed, and the production was a go. Tarantino quit Imperial.

The cast came together quickly. Hellman knew Michael

Madsen from a film called *Iguana* they made together (he auditioned for Pink but got Mr. Blonde). Eddie Bunker was a
friend of Chris Penn, but Tarantino already knew of him
because he had written the novel on which one of Tarantino's
favourite films, *Straight Time*, was based. Tim Roth came on
board, the only actor who wanted to play Mr. Orange. And
Tarantino had already sent the script to the venerable
Lawrence Tierney, a B-movie actor famous for *Dillinger*. Later,
when *Jackie Brown* came out, it was noted that Robert Forster
auditioned for the role. Samuel L. Jackson almost won the part
of Holdaway, as did Ving Rhames, but both had to wait a while
longer to enter the Tarantino universe. Tarantino apparently
wanted James Woods in the film, but miscommunication
prevailed – Woods never knew about the offer. Supposedly
George Clooney auditioned for Mr. Blonde. Meanwhile,
Keitel had bought plane tickets for Tarantino and Bender to
come to New York and meet some actors there, including
Steve Buscemi. Tarantino still planned to play Pink and may
have thought of Buscemi as Nice Guy Eddie. At some point,
Bender asked Keitel to take co-producer status.

Eventually the script was submitted to the Sundance Film
Festival for funding, and that led to an invitation to the screenplay workshop in June. The producers thought this would be a
great opportunity for Tarantino, as an untried director.
Hellman, Bender, Tarantino, and Buscemi all went to Sundance
for ten days or so, rehearsed and taped scenes, mostly the long
conversation at the film's start between Misters White and
Pink, with Tarantino playing White. Some judges were hard on
Tarantino, but Terry Gilliam, Jon Amiel, Ulu Grosbard, and
Volker Schlöndorff were nothing but encouraging and gave
him good advice, especially Gilliam.

Back in Los Angeles, three weeks before shooting, the loca-
tion scouting, rehearsals, and production meetings were under
way. On 29 July 1991 shooting began, mostly in a warehouse

that was a former mortuary at 59th and Figueroa in the Eagle Rock section of L.A. Temperatures were close to 100 degrees and the crew were using 50 A.S.A. film stock, which techies know requires a lot of lights. Meanwhile, Tarantino read a few movie disaster books, such as *Final Cut* and *The Devil's Candy*, as preparation for what might go wrong. Hellman appeared on the set about a dozen times and offered only discreet advice (he objected to the use of flatbed trucks for the car scenes because they elevated the cast unrealistically above the other traffic; he preferred that the cars be towed). In his personal life, Tarantino was breaking up with Grace Lovelace, though they got back together again for the making of his next film.

Despite numerous difficulties, the shooting of *Reservoir Dogs* sounds like fun. While planning the film, Tarantino came up with a whole new sequence (Mr. Orange narrating his story in person in the bathroom). Tarantino also had a complete shot list but enlisted first assistant director Jamie Beardsley to keep it a secret from Live because he feared he would be rigidly held accountable to the shot list, inhibiting his on-the-set creativity. There were tense moments, such as a blow-out with Tierney, but also inspired moments, as when Madsen improvised talking into the infamous severed ear.

Reservoir Dogs first appeared at Sundance on 18 January 1992. It won no awards but created intense buzz. Later, at the Toronto International Film Festival, it won an award for best first feature. In October it opened in 26 cinemas across the United States, making its money back in only ten weeks, and on 8 January 1993, it opened in Britain, where the film became a legend and Tarantino a modern cinema god.

Reservoir Dogs (1992)

Cast: Harvey Keitel (Larry Dimick/Mr. White), Tim Roth (Freddy Newandyke/Mr. Orange), Michael Madsen (Vic

Vega/Mr. Blonde), Chris Penn (Nice Guy Eddie Cabot),
Lawrence Tierney (Joe Cabot), Eddie Bunker (Mr. Blue),
Quentin Tarantino (Mr. Brown), Steven Wright (K-Billy
radio's disc jockey), Randy Brooks (Holdaway), Kirk Baltz
(Marvin Nash), Michael Sottile (Teddy), Linda Kaye (Shocked
Woman), Suzanne Celeste (Shot Woman), Lawrence Bender
(Chasing Cop and K-Billy Voice).

Crew: Producers: Lawrence Bender, Richard N. Gladstein;
Executive Producers: Monte Hellman, Harvey Keitel; Co-
producer: Ronna B. Wallace; Studio: Live Entertainment;
Theatrical Distributor: Miramax; Screenplay: Quentin
Tarantino, with additional contributions by Roger Avary;
Photography: Andrzej Sekula; Editors: Sally Menke;
Production Designer: David Wasco; Costume Designers: Betsy
Heimann, Mary Claire Hannan; Sound Editors: Stephen H.
Flick, Geoffrey G. Rubay; Casting Director: Ronnie Yeskel;
Special Effects Co-ordinator: Larry Fioritto; Running time: 99
minutes; Ratings: UK, 18; USA, R; Hong Kong, III.

Plot: Los Angeles. Present day. A jewellery shop heist has gone
terribly wrong. A gangster code-named Mr. Orange lies in the
back seat of a speeding getaway car driven by Mr. White. At the
prearranged rendezvous point, Mr. Pink, another escapee, joins
Mr. White and they attempt to piece together what happened.
The fact that police officers were waiting for them upon their
exit suggests that they have a snitch in their midst. As more of
the surviving gang members arrive, along with boss Joe 'Papa'
Cabot and his son, Nice Guy Eddie, tension increases. In a
background sequence we learn that Mr. Orange is really an
undercover cop out on his first assignment. After an overpop-
ulated Mexican standoff that leaves most of the gang slain, Mr.
Orange admits to Mr. White that in fact he is the cop who
squealed on the gang. In one interpretation of the ending, Mr.

Pink leaves with the bag of jewels only to be arrested by the police outside (or he escapes), while Mr. White slays Mr. Orange just as the police burst in and kill him.

Time Banditry: *Reservoir Dogs* is told in 'real time', an unusual approach to films seen in only a very few. Among these are Robert Wise's boxing movie *The Set-Up* (1949), Hitchcock's *Rope* (1948), *Cléo De 5 À 7* (1961), *Before Sunset* (2004), and the thriller *Nick Of Time* (1995) as well as the TV series *24*. Real time movies come closest to live theatre, yet at the same time often demand the most movie-like of camera tricks to work, as in *Rope*. It's entirely likely that many audience members might not notice the real time element of *Reservoir Dogs*. Yet concurrently, *Reservoir Dogs* also contains three jumpaways from the real-time action to fill in the backstory on the characters and let the viewer know just a little more about what's going on. Tarantino has repeatedly described these jumpaways as part of his novelistic approach to film writing, demanding the freedom that a novelist has to leap back and forth in time and approach a story at different angles with new knowledge provided to the viewer. One thing he is adamant about is that the film is not based on *The Killing*, wherein the story stops and moves back to a set starting point to resume and follow a different character, performed under the rubric of Mark Hellinger-influenced newsreel-style realism. If anything, the film more resembles *Rashômon* (1950), in which you learn more – and less – with each new segment.

Violent Moments: Yeah, sure, there are gunfights, several shootings, and an ear is sliced off. But for the most part *Reservoir Dogs* is rather talky. What stands out is the intensity of the moment that often leads to violence. Tarantino has said that 'the threat of violence is another character in the room,' and

41

this is an apt way to segregate the intensity of his movies from real, quantifiable violence.

Language: According to the Internet Movie Database, the word 'fuck' is used 252 times. Misters Pink and White use the word 'nigger' occasionally. Controversies over Tarantino's language will crop up with his later films.

Key Quote: Mr. Orange: 'What happens if the manager won't give you the diamonds?'

Mr. White: 'When you're dealing with a store like this, they're insured up the ass. They're not supposed to give you any resistance whatsoever. If you get a customer, or an employee, who thinks he's Charles Bronson, take the butt of your gun and smash their nose in. Everybody jumps. He falls down screaming, blood squirts out of his nose, nobody says fucking shit after that. You might get some bitch talk shit to you, but give her a look like you're gonna smash her in the face next, watch her shut the fuck up. Now if it's a manager, that's a different story. Managers know better than to fuck around, so if you get one that's giving you static, he probably thinks he's a real cowboy, so you gotta break that son of a bitch in two. If you wanna know something and he won't tell you, cut off one of his fingers. The little one. Then tell him his thumb's next. After that he'll tell you if he wears ladies' underwear. I'm hungry. Let's get a taco.'

Codes Of Honour: *Reservoir Dogs* manifested itself as the public's first blast of Tarantino's code of conduct, a mélange of Howard Hawks, Jean-Pierre Melville (*Le Samouraï* from 1967), Yakuza films by Kinji Fukasaku such as *Jingi Naki Tatakai* (*Battles Without Honour And Humanity*, 1973), and the ethos evinced by John Woo's Catholic-inflected films. These crooks are professionals who, despite lapses into horseplay, set about their tasks with experience and quick thinking and have contempt for those who don't act like 'a professional'. However, as seen with Mr. White and Mr. Orange, they can bond with each other despite the prohibition against self-revelation, and they act on their sense of obligation to each other, however ultimately misguided. Mr. Orange admits to Mr. White that he's a cop, sealing his own fate – but he has to do it, according to the unstated code between them. This code has a name – *yi*, an uneasily translatable Japanese term for loyalty and brotherhood.

The Tarantino Alternate Universe: Tarantino wants to interconnect his films, like the worlds that cut across several of Elmore Leonard's novels and the Glass family stories of J.D. Salinger. To that end, Tarantino holds onto the rights of all the characters in his films. Many viewers may notice that included in Tarantino's films are fake products. There is a very specific reason for this. Tarantino prefers to avoid product-placement in his movies. Thus his men smoke Red Apple cigarettes. Also, Mr. Orange eats Fruit Brute, a brand that ceased manufacture in the 1970s. Characters named Bonnie pop up in his films a lot, too. Before the *Pulp Fiction* segment *The Bonnie Situation*, Nice Guy Eddie refers to his own 'Bonnie situation' (but only in a deleted scene found on the DVD), and the implication is that this is the same Bonnie, a nurse, married to the character Jimmie Dimmick in *Pulp Fiction*. There is also an unseen Bonnie mentioned in *True Romance*. Bonnie is supposedly based on the character of Coffy in Jack Hill's 1973 film of that title who is a nurse seeking vengeance after her addicted younger sister takes some bad heroin. 'Bonnies' may have a personal relevance, since Tarantino's mother was once a nurse and has been in the medical profession. Marcellus Spivey blends Marcellus Wallace from *Pulp Fiction* and Drexl from *True*

Romance. Some listeners have heard an ad for Jack Rabbit Slim's on the radio during the torture scene.

The Music: Tarantino is famous for three things: rejuvenating the careers of old stars, his narrative disruptions, and his innovations in movie music. A large measure of Tarantino's 'hipness' comes from music use, as it does for Scorsese and Demme. Tarantino tends to use already existing pop tunes (or later, bits of scores from other movies). This is part of his philosophy of the 'movieness' of movies, that you add to the power and resonance of a moment by the emotional or ironic use of a familiar song. In his debut, Tarantino drew upon songs that he remembered from his youth in the 1970s, songs that capture the summer feel of the hot SoCal world in which these hardened professionals operate. Among the songs are Blue Swede's version of *Hooked On A Feeling*, Bedlam's version of *Magic Carpet Ride*, Harry Nilsson's *Coconut* (over the end credits), *Little Green Bag* by George Baker Selection, Joe Tex's *I Gotcha*, and *Stuck In The Middle With You* by Stealer's Wheel over the torture scene (although *Ballroom Blitz* by Sweet was almost selected). Many of these songs allude to drugs and addiction. Sandy Rogers' *Fool For Love* is perhaps the ultimate in country-western yodelling.

Magpie Moments: We will never truly know the full extent of the borrowings from films and real life that went into *Reservoir Dogs*. It's said that veterans of Video Archives, remembering old conversations held long ago in the store, can pinpoint where virtually every second came from. Still, many of the film's references are obvious. The use of colour-coded names to mask the gangsters' IDs comes from the excellent *The Taking Of Pelham One Two Three* (1974), and their mutual anonymity comes from *Kansas City Confidential* (1952). The attire of his hoods – white shirts, black suits, thin ties, sunglasses

– has two sources: John Woo's *A Better Tomorrow II* (1987) and *The Pope Of Greenwich Village* (1984); *Ocean's Eleven* (1960) and *Point Blank* (1967) might also have something to do with the look. Their exit from the diner to do the job evokes *The Wild Bunch* (1969). Godard's *Le Petit Soldat* (*The Little Soldier*, 1963) provides some inspiration for the torture scene. The 'Black women tougher than white women' speech comes from a routine by the comic Rudy Ray Moore. Other heist films important to *Reservoir Dogs* are *Plunder Road* (1957), *Bob Le Flambeur* (*Bob The Gambler*, 1955), *The Big Combo* (1955), *Du Rififi Chez Les Hommes* (*Rififi*, 1955), and *12 Angry Men* (1957). Among the many movies depicting an undercover cop betraying gangsters is *White Heat* (1949). The idea of an annoying parole officer comes from *Straight Time* (1978). The Mr. Orange death scene is borrowed from *Casualties Of War* (1989). The title of the film is said to come from Tarantino's mangling of *Au Revoir Les Enfants* (1987) and *Straw Dogs* (1971). Cited in passing in the dialogue are *Dillinger* (1945), *Honey West* (1965), and *Get Christie Love* (1974), and the comic book *The Fantastic Four* (Joe Cabot reminds comic book fan Mr. Orange of The Thing). The film is also supposed to include an example of the Willhelm Scream, which is a recording of a strange cry of pain derived from an old western that has popped up over the years in many movies, including Jackie Chan films; here it is supposed to be audible when Mr. Pink is running down the sidewalk.

But the film that *Reservoir Dogs* most resembles is *City On Fire* (1987), Ringo Lam's Hong Kong movie about an under-cover cop (Yun-Fat Chow) infiltrating a jewel-robbing gang. Comparisons between the two films were first drawn in a letter to *Asian Trash Cinema* magazine, then later in *Film Threat* and *Empire*. *Film Threat* published side-by-side frame compar-isons. Later a film buff named Mike White made a short subject comparing the two films (*Who Do You Think You're*

Fooling?). The similarities are startling, and Tarantino didn't help his case when he appeared nervous and defensive about the similarities. In fact, Tarantino appears to be doing the cinematic equivalent of hip-hop sampling techniques, but the whole subject raises complicated issues concerning intellectual property rights that will be addressed later.

Biographical Shoutouts: Back in 1984 or '85, Tarantino got into an argument with a Video Archives friend/customer named Gene Moore about tipping. Fruit Brute was Scott Spiegel's favourite cereal. Roth's vocal coach Suzanne Celeste plays the woman who shoots him as he steals her car (another regular in a similar roles is Linda Kaye). The traffic warrant tangent in Mr. Orange's tall tale reflects, according to The Mythology, some problems of Tarantino's. The K-Billy radio station first appeared in the unfinished *My Best Friend's Birthday*. The orange balloon that floats behind Nice Guy Eddie's car was a happy accident retained in the editing. Mr. Orange's apartment bears Silver Surfer posters, a Tarantino favourite, also reference in the Tarantino script-doctored dialogue in *Crimson Tide* (1995).

Alternate Versions: The movie was reduced by 15 minutes in editing (some of the footage shows up in the DVD), but producer Bender says that the existing cut is the one everyone likes. This is unconfirmed, but apparently in the Italian prints the Dogs exit the diner in regular, rather than slow, motion. Deleted scenes include the procedural sequence of a background check on Mr. White, and features what would have been the sole female speaking part (an unnamed blonde cop in a red leather jacket played by Nina Siemaszko); an argument in a car among Misters White and Pink and Nice Guy Eddie after they leave Mr. Blonde with the cop (this is the scene in which the phrase 'the Bonnie situation' first pops up); and a scene in which Mr. Orange and his supervisor discuss the hazards of an undercover assignment. There are also two takes of the ear slicing. At some point in the history of the film, a scene appeared in which Joe solicits romantic advice from Mr. Pink because Joe's girlfriend has asked him to read *The Bell Jar*. Sanjay Gupta unofficially remade the film as *Kaante* in 2002.

Foot Notes: Tarantino's character in *My Best Friend's Birthday* reveals casually that he has a foot fetish, and later the writer tried to insinuate an unwanted foot massage into *Past Midnight*. Tarantino's cinematic interest in female feet is well known, and magazines such as *Leg World* (in its June 2000 issue) suggest that the interest is more than cinematic. Peter Biskind in his book *Down And Dirty Pictures* quotes a woman named Dulce Durante, of Austin, Texas, who claims that Tarantino was fixated on her feet. In any case, in his directorial debut, Tarantino focused on a manly crew that necessarily prohibited dwelling on what is reputedly Tarantino's favourite female body part.

Nagging Questions: Who shoots Nice Guy Eddie? Does Mr. Pink escape, die, or get caught? If Mr. Pink has known Joe since he 'was a kid', why doesn't he know Mr. Blonde? Why did Mr. Orange confess to Mr. White when he didn't have to? How did Mr. Orange insinuate his way into the group in the first place? (There is a passing reference to Longbeach Mike as his sponsor.)

Critical Reaction: Critics either loved or hated *Reservoir Dogs*. Representative opinions include Kevin N. Laforest's ('riveting from start to finish') and Roger Ebert's ('Tarantino's script doesn't have much curiosity about these guys'). RottenTomatoes.com gave it a 93 per cent 'fresh' rating.

Release Dates: In the United States, the film came out on Friday, 23 October 1992, and in the UK on 8 January 1993.

Box Office: With a budget of $1.6 million, *Reservoir Dogs* went on to make $2.8 million in the United States, then £10 million in Britain and an additional $20 million worldwide. The subsequent videotape sold 900,000 units in the United States.

Awards: Prix Tournage at the Avignon Film Festival; Best Director and Best Screenplay at the Catalonian International Film Festival, Sitges, Spain; Steve Buscemi, Best Supporting Male, Independent Spirit Awards; Tarantino, Newcomer of the Year, London Critics Circle Film Awards; Harvey Keitel, Best Foreign Actor, Sant Jordi Awards; Tarantino, Bronze Horse, Stockholm Film Festival; Tarantino, International Critics Award, Toronto International Film Festival.

The DVD: In the US, Live Entertainment (now Artisan) released the DVD on 17 June 1997. That disc was superseded in 2002 by a tenth anniversary two-disc edition with novelty packaging (five box cover choices) and numerous supplements (an edited commentary track, deleted scenes, Sundance workshop footage, video interviews, and numerous other features). The set famously had some sound problems, however, and a washed-out image. In November 2000 Momentum Pictures released a DVD of *Reservoir Dogs* in the UK, supplemented with an intro by Tarantino, and that was followed in June 2004 by a special edition, similar to the US edition though with a better transfer (but still some sound issues).

Evaluation: *Reservoir Dogs* is an assured directorial debut. It is sharp, bright, engrossing, well acted, and creatively shot, edited, and structured. It takes a care-worn genre and polishes it for public consumption.

The film also established a number of what would later become Tarantino signatures, among them a reputation as a 'comeback creator,' or revitalizer of an older actor's career, an omnivorous absorption of films past, the introduction of novelistic techniques into screenplays, and a redefinition of what is cool by blending Rat Pack culture with the new Cocktail Nation.

How did he do it? How did a young man who had barely written anything and not really directed anything manage to turn out such a ravishing debut film? I believe there are three reasons: One, after Tarantino's friend Spiegel was fired from a movie he was making called *The Nutty Nut*, Tarantino was also worried about getting fired from his own film. Bender advised the neophyte to put all the conventional shots at the start of the schedule, and save the complex material for the end of the shoot so the investors would be reassured. Second, Bender and Hellman made Tarantino compile a shot list, which they worked on for two weeks at Hellman's house. This was invaluable in keeping the shoot on schedule. Finally, at Sundance, Terry Gilliam gave Tarantino good advice, which may sound obvious but can be easily forgotten by filmmakers who view themselves as *auteurs* with no foundation: that was to learn how to delegate. The set decorators, costumers, and other craftspeople are there to help the director achieve his vision. Tarantino, apparently, saw the sense of that early, and it perhaps freed him to concentrate on his themes and obsessions and nail them down more strongly than would the usual debutant director.

These themes are threefold and have been little explored in writings on Tarantino's work – but they all got their start here. They include gangsterism as performance art, the use of actual dogs in *Reservoir Dogs*, and the role of luck and fate.

'Movies', according to Godard, 'must have a beginning, a middle, and an end, but not necessarily in that order.' That may have been the most influential statement Tarantino ever heard, and his readings of Elmore Leonard only encouraged the budding screenwriter to think novelistically. The thing is, gangster and crime films (like horror films and other 'low-class' genre products) lend themselves more easily to playing with time and the shuffling of story elements. There are exceptions (*Citizen Kane*, *The Hours*), but for the most part the 'tradition of quality' in Hollywood prefers a rather bland, straightforward surface.

The modern vogue for disrupted narratives starts with *Reservoir Dogs*. It's rewarding to compare the groundbreaking *Reservoir Dogs* to another film released around the same time that also augured a new directorial talent and signalled the revitalization of *noir* and crime films as a proper playing field of mature talents: *The Usual Suspects* (1995). In certain ways *The Usual Suspects* strives for exactly the density of story whose absence Tarantino bemoaned in numerous interviews. The story of an *ad hoc* coalition of crooks who pull a successful revenge job, the narrative takes them from New York City to Los Angeles to San Francisco in a sometimes convoluted path that shows a surprising variety of terrain, like *Out Of The Past*, another *noir* that surprises the viewer with its amount of sunlight and globe-hopping. Like the later *Memento*, *The Usual Suspects* plays with time, but in a way different from Tarantino. Like *Memento*, the film's conclusion demands that the viewer rethink all that has gone before, then realize the story was different than the one they thought they were viewing, hidden in plain sight. *Reservoir Dogs* is interested in the revelation of character and how that changes the way the moviegoer has understood what they've seen.

In the end, *The Usual Suspects* is a film more written than directed. In fact, writer Christopher McQuarrie's next film, the masterly *The Way Of The Gun*, was much more 'Tarantinoesque,' with its dedication to masculine codes, blundering and fate, subtle filmic references and criminal milieu. Significantly, though, the film's two pals have an admirably wordless rapport with each other, and the movie ends with citations to Sam Peckinpah, a director from whom Tarantino always distances himself.

What differentiates Tarantino's films from his numerous imitators is that his gangsters are aware of performance as an essential tool of their trade. 'Let's get into character,' Jules says, as they are about to confront a room of men in *Pulp Fiction*. 'Did I play my part right?' Alabama asks Clarence in *True Romance*. And in *Reservoir Dogs*, one of the themes is instruction in how to behave, how to act. It's as if all the characters were imagined by sociologist Erving Goffman, who specialized in charting the unstated rules that dictate our public 'performances' with each other (like Tarantino, Goffman was especially interested in diners).

Mr. White gives Mr. Orange a crash course in dealing with a room of jewelery store employees. Holdaway even gives Mr. Orange a script to memorize. In one of the film's most brilliant sequences, indeed, one of the most brilliant scenes in all '90s cinema, Mr. Orange tells his story, and the film advances through time as he improves his de Livery, presents it to the gang (as an 'audition') and then 'lives' this fable. This narrative trick is on the order of one of John Le Carré's brilliant multilayered investigations, such as when Smiley retraces the steps of Vladimir in *Smiley's People*. Goffman would have been especially interested in the subtle differences between the manufactured story that Mr. Orange tells and the supposedly 'real' story that Nice Guy Eddie tells in the car about E-Lois, really an elaborate prelude to a punch line. Mr. Orange is convincing when he tells his tale, but that is because he has rehearsed it. But when he denies being a snitch, he lacks conviction, or Goffman's attribute of unforced (but faked) sincerity.

By implication, this sequence raises the interesting, almost existential question of just who exactly 'tells' a movie. What is the movie equivalent of the literary 'I'? Where is the first person 'located' in the nexus of story, image and sound? What can be marvellous about movies is that the 'I' can shift, and Tarantino is on to that, giving his films weird depths. Godard also said that his films were documentaries about actors playing roles, and Tarantino, an actors' director, brings an enthusiasm for 'great parts' that leads him to crime as the optimal terrain. For him, gangsters are the equivalent of the great directors he loves. Within his films Tarantino's stand-ins, such as Mr. Orange, represent struggling young filmmakers trying to learn the trade. It's a situation you also see later between The Bride and Bill in *Kill Bill*. Even Mr. White (Keitel) has a father figure, but when White becomes a mentor to Orange, Joe Cabot is betrayed, which leads to White's betrayal of his own mentor.

So who are the dogs in *Reservoir Dogs*? It's known that as a kid Tarantino had two beloved pet canines, and dogs figure in the film as a sub-theme, such as in Mr. Blonde's challenge, 'Are you gonna bark all day, little doggie, or are you gonna bite?' and in the drug-sniffing dogs in the 'commode story.' Dogs may well represent that which on the surface looks nice, appealing and comfortable but which can turn on you (like Mr. Blonde) irrationally. Tarantino is attracted, among other things, to the insanity beneath the bland surface, both in the movies he likes and the movies he makes.

He is also attracted to the team of professionals, loyalty (and betrayal) amongst colleagues, and the weight of obligations to others. What messes up these principles, at least in *Reservoir Dogs* is fate (a phrase prominent in *NBK*), and just plain bad luck. Mr. White is the bad luck boy of this movie. He was just in a job where an undercover cop spoiled the heist (in a deleted scene we learn that he killed the rat and a bunch of other cops). Now it's happening again. And for the same reason? Letting friendship blind him to the truth? But bad luck permeates the film. When Joe Cabot asks Mr. White why one Marcellus Spivey is in the slammer, Mr. White replies, 'Bad luck.' Striving to escape your current state, to improve yourself, is another theme of the movie, and that's Mr. Orange's story, a cop who wants advancement. His desire for it becomes Mr. White's bad luck.

Here's a final example of *Reservoir Dog's* enduring power. During my preparation to write this portion of the book, I gathered several other film buffs and Tarantino admirers at a fellow film geek's house (he had better technology). I went with the expectation that, since we had all seen the film before many times, we would all chat about it, comment on it, and that I would gather up their critical droppings and use them as my own. But about halfway through the movie, we realized that we hadn't said a word. From the second the DVD started we were rapt, once again engrossed in *Reservoir Dogs'* taut narrative, precise framing, and its '70s exploitation-film SoCal sunshine look. *5/5*

3. Pulp Fame

Pairing *True Romance* and *Natural Born Killers* for this chapter is entirely appropriate – they had their genesis within the same screenplay.

Called *The Open Road*, that ur-script was written by Roger Avary in 1985 when he was 19 and later revised by Tarantino after Avary showed it to him in 1987 (the title comes from Kerouac). Their plan was to shoot the script on 16mm for $60,000 – guerrilla filmmaking style. Under Tarantino's refurbishment, however, and with the help of Craig Hamann, the script blossomed to some 500 pages.

The Open Road in its original conception, according to The Mythology, told the parallel or mirroring stories of Clarence and Alabama, young lovers on the road (the part written by Tarantino), and Mickey and Mallory Knox, a murderous married couple who attract a lot of media attention (the original Avary draft) and were the subject of a script that Clarence was writing.

Unable to get that script turned into a movie, Tarantino yanked *The Open Road* apart. He created a discrete unit called *True Romance*, which he intended as his directorial debut. When, over the course of several years, that project stumbled, he focused on the remaining portion of the screenplay and called it *Natural Born Killers*. When that one failed to fly, he turned instead to *Reservoir Dogs*.

This is probably the junction at which to comment on what

Hollywood writer-directors mean when they say they 'wrote' something. What comes to my mind and probably yours when someone says they are 'writing' is an image of someone sitting before a computer or typewriter and banging out prose, looking up words in a dictionary, checking the spelling of a performer's name, revising, reshaping, printing it out and doing it all over again.

This is not necessarily what writer-directors mean by 'writing.' Howard Hawks deemed himself a writer when he wrote out a few pages of text on a yellow legal pad early in the morning on the set. Billy Wilder dictated his scripts, and a pool of secretaries at Paramount typed them up in the appropriate format. John Huston gave a copy of *The Maltese Falcon* to his secretary and told her to type out the dialogue; Welles could take a book like, say, *The Magnificent Ambersons*, cross out parts he wanted deleted, and give that to a secretary. Not for these men, then, the tedious tabbing and spacing that makes screenplay formatting discouraging to naïve neophytes.

The Mythology acknowledges that Tarantino usually writes in high school spiral notebooks and then gives the notebooks to someone else – usually a good friend such as Hamann – to type, shape, and format. Avary has noted that Tarantino can't spell very well and even writes out the English language phonetically.

There is nothing necessarily wrong with any of these deviations from what we customarily call 'writing'. Writer-directors simply have a different definition. In their view, if they merely think up something, they have 'written' it, even if the result is the product of someone else's toil at the keyboard.

In any case Avary, Hamann, and Tarantino finished *True Romance* in 1988. This time, though, they decided to not make it guerrilla style, and to that end searched the Video Archives customer database for likely investors. Meanwhile, Cathryn Jaymes gave the script to British accountant turned

Hollywood business manager Stanley Margolis, who had moved to the United States in 1976. Margolis had moved into producing (*Ball Bearing Boogie*, *The Dark Is Mine*) made a commitment to the film to the extent that, according to The Mythology, he even mortgaged his house.

But every production company in town turned down the script, the inexperienced Tarantino's attachment as director being one of the reasons. After he was convinced to step aside as director, Margolis approached William Lustig (*Maniac Cop* and now the owner of the DVD company Blue Underground). Lustig's views on the script conflicted with Tarantino's; he wanted to change the ending so that Clarence lives.

And it turns out that he wasn't the only one who wanted the ending rewritten: others included some potential foreign distributors. Tarantino refused to do it, so Avary wrote the happy ending, also adding a voice-over for Alabama at the beginning and end. In a complex chain of ownership the script appears to have passed from Lustig to Paris-based producer Samuel Hadida, who in 1991 paid off Lustig and took the script to Gregory Cascante's August Entertainment.

By this time Tarantino was working at Cine-Tel. Also employed there was Stacey Sher. She had once worked for Tony Scott (one of the vocal Tarantino's favourite directors). Sher had been invited to Scott's birthday party (his birthday is 21 July) and took Tarantino along. The young man impressed Scott, who asked to look at his scripts. Tarantino sent him *True Romance* and *Reservoir Dogs*. Scott apparently wanted to shoot both of them, but by this time Tarantino was putting together *Reservoir Dogs* for himself. Scott settled for *True Romance*, although at one point, according to The Mythology, Scott and his partner Bill Unger asked Tarantino if he wanted to direct with Scott producing.

Meanwhile, Cascante approached Miramax, which was interested in the project when it was a $6 million movie. But with Scott it was becoming a $25 million movie and the company begged off. Morgan Creek stepped up, offering a sum on delivery of the film in return for distribution rights in the US and UK Hadida and Cascante got Banque Paribas to provide production funds, and shooting began on 15 September 1992.

Natural Born Killers, finished in 1989, had an equally complex path to the screen. Cathryn Jaymes sent around the script to potential filmmakers or agents, often eliciting violent rejections. According to different versions of The Mythology, Tarantino washed his hands of this script in summer 1991, first giving it to pal Rand Vossler and later selling an option on it to Jane Hamsher and Don Murphy, neophyte producers just out of film school. Murphy apparently met Tarantino through Video Archives and Vossler (Hamsher later went on to produce the Alan Moore adaptation, *From Hell* while Murphy did *League Of Extraordinary Gentlemen*).

NBK's subsequent torturous route to the screen as an Oliver Stone movie has been chronicled in Hamsher's book *Killer Instinct*, an account (not of the Mythology school) of her and Murphy's work on the film, and mostly about Oliver Stone and his company (though obviously Tarantino figures in it). Hamsher and Murphy had originally accepted Vossler as the director but then fired him and ended up settling a lawsuit with him over ownership of the script. Meanwhile, according to them, Tarantino attempted to block the production and later interfered with the film by discouraging actors under his influence from taking parts (Michael Madsen was one of the actors offered the part of Mickey).

Aside from a bizarre excursion in which Avary was enlisted to write a scene for the bodybuilders David and Peter Paul, who promised to help finance the film, the script made its way from Sean Penn (considered for director) to producer Thom Mount, thence to Stone.

True Romance did poorly at the box office but developed a cult following. *Natural Born Killers* was profitable, controversial, and a bellwether for pundits gnawing on the subject of violence in the media. But despite their convoluted production histories and varied receptions, the two films provided another one-two punch that further enhanced Tarantino's reputation as viewers waited for his inevitable follow-up to *Reservoir Dogs*.

True Romance (1993)

Cast: Christian Slater (Clarence Worley), Patricia Arquette (Alabama Whitman), Dennis Hopper (Clifford Worley), Val Kilmer (Clarence's Imaginary Mentor, Elvis), Gary Oldman (Drexl Spivey), Brad Pitt (Floyd), Christopher Walken (Vincenzo Coccotti), Bronson Pinchot (Elliot Blitzer), Samuel L. Jackson (Big Don), Michael Rapaport (Dick Ritchie), Saul Rubinek (Lee Donowitz), Conchata Ferrell (Mary Louise Ravencroft), James Gandolfini (Virgil), Chris Penn (Nicky Dimes), Tom Sizemore (Cody Nicholson), Kevin Corrigan (Marvin), Jack Black (Movie Theatre Usher in a deleted scene), Ed Lauter (Police Capt. Quiggle), Enzo Rossi (Alabama and Clarence's Son, Elvis).

Crew: Director: Tony Scott; Producers: Gary Barber, Steve Perry, Samuel Hadida, Bill Unger; Co-producers: Don Edmonds, James W. Skotchdopole; Associate Producers: Lisa Cogswell, Spencer Franklin, Gregory S. Manson; Executive Producers: James G. Robinson, Bob Weinstein, Harvey Weinstein; Studio: Warner Bros./Morgan Creek; Screenplay: Quentin Tarantino; Story: from earlier script elements by Roger Avary, Quentin Tarantino; Photography: Jeffrey L. Kimball; Editors: Michael Tronick, Christian Wagner; Original Music: Hans Zimmer; Production Designer: Benjamín

Fernández; Costume Designer: Susan Becker; Sound Editors: Bub Asman; Casting Directors: Risa Bramon Garcia, Billy Hopkins; Special Effects Co-ordinators: Robert Henderson, Larry Shorts; Unusual Credits: The owner of the coffee shop is listed as Coffee Shop (because of his dialogue), and Emil Sitka is listed as 'Hold Hands, You Love Birds!' Running time: 120 minutes; Ratings: UK, 18; USA, R.

Plot: Detroit. Present day. Clarence Worley, a clerk in a comic book store, is celebrating his birthday by trying to pick up a woman in a bar and bring her to see a Sonny Chiba triple bill with him. Failing that, he goes to the cinema alone and there meets Alabama Whitney. After an emotional night of intimacy, Alabama admits that Clarence's boss, Lance, hired her to get him laid. Instead she found that she really loves him. They marry the next morning. Unfortunately, Alabama has a pimp, Drexl, and Clarence gets it into his head to free her from Drexl's domination. Giving the excuse that he's just going over to pick up her things, Clarence soon confronts Drexl, and the experienced pimp is chagrined to find that he has underestimated the otherwise nerdy clerk. Clarence kills Drexl and his assistant and flees with what he thinks is Alabama's suitcase but which is really filled with cocaine. The couple flees from the city to Hollywood, where, with the help of aspiring actor friend Dick Ritchie, they will peddle the cocaine, first stopping off to visit Clarence's father, Cliff. Hard on their heels, however, are the gangsters Drexl worked for, led by Vincenzo Coccotti. Coccotti arrives at Cliff's trailer and tortures him to unearth Clarence's whereabouts. Cliff, however, manipulates Coccotti into killing him before Cliff can reveal the information. The gangsters find it anyway. They arrive in Los Angeles not long after Clarence has hooked up with Ritchie, who connects them to Elliot Blitzer, personal assistant to action movie producer Lee Donowitz, who decides to buy the dope.

After Alabama narrowly escapes death from Virgil, one of Coccotti's henchmen, she, Clarence, and Ritchie meet with Donowitz at the Beverly Ambassador Hotel. Unknown to them, however, Blitzer, arrested on a separate charge, has agreed to wear a wire to the meeting to avoid prosecution. Independent of that, the gangsters have also learned of Clarence's whereabouts. All converge on the hotel room for a shootout, in which only Ritchie, Alabama, and Clarence (barely) survive, the couple getting away with a suitcase of cash. In a coda, the viewer learns that Clarence and Alabama have settled in Cancun, Mexico, and have had a child, named after Clarence's hero, Elvis.

Time Banditry: The most famous aspect to *True Romance*'s time disjunctions is that they did not survive from script to screen. In Tarantino's version, the movie begins with Clarence in the bar, then jumps to Drexl murdering some guys for drugs, then to Clarence and Alabama with Cliff (with a side intro of Dick Ritchie), and then forward to Clarence with Ritchie in Hollywood, where Clarence tells in flashback what is now the second sequence of the film, with narration added. Tarantino protested about the changes to Tony Scott, but now, according to interviews, accepts the chronological version with the happy ending as perfect for Scott's film.

Violent Moments: The violent high points are the fight between Clarence and Drexl and the battle between Alabama and Virgil. The second of Tarantino's many Mexican standoffs occurs in the hotel room climax.

Language: The word 'nigger' is used liberally in the famous Sicilian speech (as follows).

Key Quote:

Clifford Worley:	'You're Sicilian, huh?'
Coccotti:	'Yeah, Sicilian.'
Clifford:	'You know, I read a lot, especially about things about history. I find that shit fascinating. Here's a fact I don't know whether you know or not. Sicilians were spawned by niggers.'
Coccotti:	'Come again?'
Clifford:	'It's a fact. Yeah. You see, uh, Sicilians have, uh, black blood pumping through their hearts. Hey, no, if eh, if eh, if you don't believe me, uh, you can look it up. Hundreds and hundreds of years ago, uh, you see, uh, the Moors conquered Sicily. And the Moors are niggers.'
Coccotti:	'Yes.'
Clifford:	'So you see, way back then, uh, Sicilians were like, uh, wops from Northern Italy. Ah, they all had blonde hair and blue eyes, but, uh, well, then the Moors moved in there, and uh, well, they changed the whole country. They did so much fuckin' with Sicilian women – huh? – that they changed the whole bloodline forever. That's why blonde hair and blue eyes became black hair and dark skin. You know, it's absolutely amazing to me to think that to this day, hundreds of years later, that, uh, that Sicilians still carry that nigger gene. Now this . . . [*Coccotti laughs*] No, I'm,

	no, I'm quoting . . . history. It's written. It's a fact, it's written.'
Coccotti [*laughing*]:	'I love this guy.'
Clifford:	'Your ancestors are niggers. Uh-huh. Hey. Yeah. And, and your great-great-great-great grandmother fucked a nigger, yeah, and she had a half-nigger kid. Now, if that's a fact, tell me, am I lying?'

Codes Of Honour: There are two important acts of sacrifice, and they both have ironic consequences. First, Cliff, trying to buy time for his son, tells the Sicilian story in an attempt to make Coccotti so mad that he will kill Cliff, which he does. Later, Alabama also attempts a sacrifice, when Virgil tracks her to a motel. She tries to postpone telling Virgil anything for as long as she can, almost to the point of death. Then she manages to kill Virgil. The paradox is that in both cases the thing sought (Clarence's address in Hollywood, the suitcase full of cocaine) is right there in the open and easily found despite the sacrifices, one of them mortal.

The Tarantino Alternate Universe: This is a Tony Scott film, and in any case the script was written when Tarantino hadn't yet geared up the creation of his unique world. Still, Alabama as a character is also mentioned in *Reservoir Dogs*. One of the movies that Donowitz has produced is the Vietnam war epic *Comin' Home In A Body Bag*.

The Music: About 20 songs are used in the film, chosen of course, by Scott's team, though a few of them, such as *A Little Bitty Tear* by Burl Ives and the Big Bopper's *Chantilly Lace*, were written into the script, and Scott honoured that. Other key tunes include Charlie Sexton's *Graceland* and The Shirelles'

Will You Love Me Tomorrow? Sous Le Dôme Épais Où Le Blanc Jasmin from the opera *Lakmé*, composed by Léo Delibes, is used behind Cliff's death scene. Val Kilmer does a little bit of *Heartbreak Hotel*.

Magpie Moments: Several movies are mentioned in passing: *Mr. Majestyk* (1974, which also figures in *Kill Bill*), *Bullitt* (1968) as if it were a TV show, *Apocalypse Now* (1979), the TV shows *The Partridge Family* and *T. J. Hooker*, and *Doctor Zhivago* (1965), used as a code name for cocaine (because there is a lot of snow in the movie). The titles of some are incorporated into the dialogue (Kubrick's *Fear And Desire*, from 1953). When Clarence confronts Drexl, *The Mack* (1973, and one of Tarantino's favourite blaxploitation movies) is playing on the tube and also figures in the dialogue. In the original script Clarence specifically talks about Elvis in *Jailhouse Rock* (1957) when we first encounter him. The triple bill of Sonny Chiba films that figure in the meeting of Clarence and Alabama are *Gekitotsu! Satsujin Ken* (*The Streetfighter*, 1974), *Satsujin Ken 2* (*Return Of The Streetfighter*, 1974), and *Onna Hissatsu Ken* (*Sister Streetfighter*, 1974). In general the film evokes previous couple-on-the-run films, from *Badlands* (1973) to David Lynch's *Wild At Heart* (1990). Clarence's 'rescue' of Alabama seems inspired at least partially by *Taxi Driver* (1976), and the Mexico-bound ending is reminiscent of *The Getaway* (1972). In the background on the walls of Dick Ritchie's apartment are several movie posters, including one for *Highway 301*, a film that Tarantino happens to like, but its presence was not dictated by the script (Tarantino dismisses the posters in the room as inappropriately and overly 'set designed').

Biographical Shoutouts: Many elements from the earlier *My Best Friend's Birthday* are incorporated into *True Romance*. They include the hooker birthday present idea as well as that of the pimp who dominates her. Clarence's comicbook store is a good stand-in for Video Archives, also owned by someone named Lance. Clarence's speech about living near the airport reflects Tarantino's own experience, as does Dick Ritchie's casting calls. A speech that Clarence makes to Cliff (named after Tarantino's uncle by marriage) reflects what he did or might have said to Curt Zastoupil. The Sicilian story comes from a man named Don, now dead, who was the brother of one of his mother's boyfriends. According to his audio track on the DVD, Don told Tarantino that he was glad the truth finally came out in that picture.

Alternate Versions: As complex as the production history of the film are its different versions. Initially, the US and foreign versions were cut, mostly losing bits from the fight between Alabama and Virgil. However, a complete, unrated version became available on DVD in the US. In the UK, the theatrical and video releases were the R-rated US version, until August 1999, when the British Board of Film Classification gave the longer director's cut an 18 Certificate for video release.

Foot Notes: Apparently not having a foot fetish, Scott includes no special emphasis on anyone's extremities, despite the script's call for a photo of a ballet dancer's feet on the wall of Dick Ritchie's apartment.

Nagging Questions: Why isn't Ritchie, an actor, absorbing all that he sees around him? Who is Slater imitating, Jack Nicholson, or Elvis?

Critical Reaction: Reviews were 85 per cent positive, with the *Austin Chronicle* calling it 'consistently entertaining' and Roger Ebert writing that the film was 'made with such energy, such high spirits, such an enchanting goofiness, that it's impossible to resist.' *Boxoffice* magazine called the film 'even more impressive' than *Reservoir Dogs*.

Release Dates: 10 September 1993, in the US, 15 October in the UK.

Box Office: With a budget of $12.5 million, *True Romance* made a disappointing $12.2 million in the United States.

Awards: Three various nominations but no wins.

The DVD: The director's cut enjoyed laser disc release in January 1994. It was one of the earliest films released in the new DVD format in September 1997. Warner Home Entertainment released a subsequent two-disc DVD set in September 2002 that offered the director's cut and numerous deleted or expanded scenes, plus three audio commentary tracks (Slater and Arquette, Scott, and finally Tarantino in an insightful track in which he gives what could be called the quintessential Tarantino performance). In the UK the director's cut was released in April 2000.

Evaluation: *True Romance* is obviously Tarantino's 'Elmore Leonard' movie, not just because it starts out in Detroit and makes references to Miami, the opposing poles of the Leonardian world, but also because the film has the intricacy of a typical Leonard novel, in which competing criminals are at odds with each other, sometimes unknowingly – and Tarantino has often said in interviews that one of the things he wants to bring to his films is the freedom novelists like Leonard enjoy.

Tarantino's *True Romance* would no doubt have been much different from Scott's, but still the script is consistent with Tarantino's other films. It continues the dominant theme of his work, of everyday life as performance. 'Did I play my part right?' Alabama asks after one excursion, and overall Clarence is acting his way through the adventure, based on movies he has seen and on what Elvis might do.

Also consistent with other Tarantino moments is Alabama saying that she likes to eat pie after a movie (see *Pulp Fiction*). Trailers (*Kill Bill*), motels (*From Dusk Till Dawn*, *Pulp Fiction*), and convertibles (*Natural Born Killers*, *Kill Bill*) are common living spaces. And, as will be shown in *Pulp Fiction*, Clarence, like Vince Vega, has a habit of going to the bathroom at inopportune times, emerging to find himself plunged into chaos. And Vietnam figures tangentially in the tale (*Pulp Fiction*).

But there is trouble in paradise. In a brief audio commentary on the 2002 US DVD, Brad Pitt makes an interesting, apologetically delivered observation. He says that when he first read the screenplay he 'didn't get it.' He didn't understand why the father was killed and then never mentioned again, he didn't grasp the tone, and he didn't comprehend the point of Clarence. These are noteworthy points because they get at the heart of what ultimately is wrong with *True Romance*, enjoyable as it is. Clarence is a fantasy figure of a nerd. He starts out a geeky clerk in a comic book store and then rather quickly becomes an omni-competent Charles Bronson clone. His switch from dork to he-man is not fully motivated, if it is motivated at all. After he kills Drexl, Clarence becomes something of a remote figure in the movie. The emotional centre shifts to Alabama, but her love for Clarence, though uplifting, doesn't seem justifiably inspired. Still, *True Romance* has many excellent moments and a great cast and is yet another stylish and involving Tony Scott film. *3/5*

Natural Born Killers (1994)

Cast: Woody Harrelson (Mickey Knox), Juliette Lewis (Mallory Knox), Robert Downey, Jr. (Wayne Gale), Tommy

Lee Jones (Warden Dwight McClusky), Tom Sizemore (Jack Scagnetti), Rodney Dangerfield (Ed Wilson, Mallory's Dad), Edie McClurg (Mallory's Mom), Corinna Everson (TV Mallory), Dale Dye (Dale Wrigley), Evan Handler (David), Corinna Laszlo (Emily, Hostage in Motel), Balthazar Getty (Gas Station Attendant), Red West (Cowboy Sheriff), Russell Means (Old Indian), Pruitt Taylor Vince (Kavanaugh), Steven Wright (Dr. Emil Reingold), Ashley Judd (Grace Mulberry, scene deleted), David and Peter Paul (The Hun Brothers, scene deleted), James Gammon (Redneck's Buddy in the Diner), Jennifer Say Gan (Asian Reporter), Jane Hamsher (Female Demon), Mark Harmon (Mickey Knox in Wayne Gale's Reconstruction), Arliss Howard (Owen Traft), Denis Leary (Prison Inmate, director's cut), Don Murphy (Prison Guard), Richard Rutowski (Prisoner with Mustache), Rachel Ticotin (Prosecutor Wanda Bisbing, director's cut).

Crew: Director: Oliver Stone; Producers: Jane Hamsher, Don Murphy, Clayton Townsend; Co-producer: Rand Vossler; Associate Producers: Risa Bramon Garcia, Richard Rutowski; Executive Producers: Arnon Milchan, Thom Mount; Studio: Warner Bros.; Screenplay: David Veloz, Richard Rutowski, Oliver Stone; Story: from a screenplay by Quentin Tarantino; Photography: Robert Richardson; Editors: Brian Berdan, Hank Corwin; Original Music: Brent Lewis, Trent Reznor; Production Designer: Victor Kemptser; Costume Designer: Richard Hornung; Sound Editor: Robert Batha; Casting Directors: Risa Bramon Garcia, Billy Hopkins, Heidi Levitt; Special Effects Co-ordinator: Matt Sweeney; Running time: 118 minutes; Ratings: UK, R; HK, III.

Plot: American Southwest. A diner. Present day. Mickey Knox is having breakfast and his girlfriend, Mallory Knox, is at the jukebox flirting. With typical unexpectedness, the pair fly into a rage and kill the staff and customers, leaving one person alive to tell what he saw. In a flashback we learn that Mallory was an abused daughter and Mickey was the meat deliverer with whom she developed a preternatural bond. Mickey rescues Mallory, killing her father and burning down the house. After performing an unofficial wedding ceremony the pair embark on a crime spree that attracts national attention, especially through the reality TV show *American Maniacs*, whose host is the Australian personality Wayne Gale. Also on their trail is Detective Jack Scagnetti. The couple have a brief falling out over a hostage, after which the Knoxes seek redemption in the desert through the services of an Indian shaman. However, Mickey kills the shaman while in a state of paranoid intoxication. Finally, Scagnetti and the police catch up with the Knoxes at a 24-hour drugstore. Held in separate sections of the same prison, Mickey and Mallory are being set up for private execution by the prison warden, using Scagnetti. But on the day Scagnetti arrives, Wayne Gale enters the prison with his crew to tape one last interview, to be aired during half-time on Super Bowl Sunday. Mickey turns the tables on his executioners and rescues Mallory just as she is about to be raped by Scagnetti. Leaving the prison in chaos, Mickey and Mallory drive off with Gale, pausing only to execute their hostage on camera. In a phantasmagoric coda Mickey and Mallory are shown living their lives as a happy domestic couple having given up their life of crime.

Time Banditry: The film begins *in medias res* and then tells the couple's backstory via the show *American Maniacs*. But aside from that, all through the film, thanks to Stone's jagged editing style, even the smallest events come at you as pulses, a character showing one emotion, then its opposite in quick succession. But again, that is a Stone thing, not a Tarantino thing.

Violent Moments: There are almost too many to list, and most of them are overdone, poetic and are presented in several media ('reality' and animation at the same time, say). But key moments include the diner scene at the beginning, the murder of Mallory's dad, the killing of the gas station attendant, and the chaos of the prison break at the end.

Language: Surprisingly, the least troublesome aspect of the film is its language. It's probably the tamest of any Tarantino script.

Key Quote: Mickey: 'It's fate, you know. Nobody can stop fate, nobody can.'

Codes Of Honour: The nobility of the love between Mickey and Mallory during their three-week, 52-victim killing spree is arguably what Tarantino may have found the most alluring element of the film as he conceived it (derived as it is from Roger Avary's original). It's an adolescent vision of romantic loyalty, but one that has elements of John Milius in it, for which see *Big Wednesday*, another one of Tarantino's favourite movies, in which a husband and wife talk about fighting for each other: 'If they dragged me away would you come get me?' (at 19:41 on the US DVD).

The Tarantino Alternate Universe: Again, this category doesn't really apply because it is more an Oliver Stone movie. However, Mickey does refer to Mallory once as 'Honey Bunny.' Also, the pie business crops up again with Mickey saying, 'Well, let's give that key lime pie a day in court.'

The Music: There are more than 70 music cues in *Natural Born Killers*, ranging from three songs by Leonard Cohen to bits from *Wozzeck* (by Alban Berg), *Madame Butterfly* (Puccini), and *A Night On Bare Mountain* by Modest Mussorgsky. Also included are *Shitlist* by L7, *Leader Of The Pack* by The Shangri-las, *Rock 'N' Roll Nigger* by Patti Smith, *Sweet Jane* by Cowboy Junkies, *Ted Just Admit It* by Jane's Addiction, and pieces by Diamanda Galas, Nine Inch Nails, Peter Gabriel, Marilyn Manson, Dr. Dre, Rage Against The Machine, and Spore. Juliette Lewis even sings *These Boots Are Made For Walking* to herself at one point.

Magpie Moments: Stone doesn't go in for as much New Wave cinematic quotation as Tarantino. *Lost Horizon* (1937) and *Serpico* (1973) are cited in the dialogue. *Bonnie And Clyde* (1967) and *Badlands* (1973), as violent couple-on-the-run movies, are important to its existence, with Mickey's murder of Mallory's father an echo of Martin Sheen's actions in *Badlands*. In general *NBK* evokes *C'est Arrivé Près De Chez Vous*, otherwise known as *Man Bites Dog* (1992). There is also a magical component to the film that evokes *The Wizard Of Oz* (1939). Bits of several films are also discernible: *Frankenstein* (1931), *Triumph Of The Will* (1934), *The Wild Bunch* (1969), *Midnight Express* (1978), and *Scarface* (1983), the latter pair written by Stone, and the TV series *77 Sunset Strip*. Stone, however, quotes from himself frequently, including a music cue at the start of the prison sequence that sounds a lot like the cue when Garrison arrives at the prison in *JFK*.

Biographical Shoutouts: None

Alternate Versions: Again, the complexity of the production history is matched only by the multiplicity of versions of this highly censored film. In general the director's cut has more violence, such as the image of the prison warden's head on a pike. There is an alternate ending, however, wherein Owen, a character who helps Mickey and Mallory escape from prison, turns on them and kills the couple. The director's cut also restores wholly deleted scenes, such as a short sequence with Denis Leary.

Foot Notes: At one point Juliette Lewis sticks her feet straight up and rests them on the top of the windshield of the couple's convertible, but overall feet aren't Stone's thing.

Nagging Questions: What is the time frame of the story? How has Scagnetti managed to survive this long in law enforcement? What happened to the hostage in the motel room?

Critical Reaction: *NBK* was one of the most controversial films of the 1990s. Some critics denounced its politics, others swooned over its technical innovations. And they appear to be almost evenly divided – the film receives a 53 per cent 'rotten' rating from RottenTomatoes.com.

Release Dates: 26 August 1994 in the US; 24 February 1995 in the UK.

Box Office: With a budget of $35 million, *Natural Born Killers* went on to make a misleading (misleading, that is, given the amount of media attention it received as the film entered the national debate on violence) $50.2 in the United States, $2.6 million in the UK and over $100 million worldwide.

Awards: Best Actress award for Juliette Lewis and the Special Jury Prize for Oliver Stone at the Venice Film Festival.

The DVD: The director's cut was first released by Trimark in January 2000 because Warner Home Entertainment, at least at that time, didn't distribute unrated or NC-17 movies.

However, an expanded version of the R-rated disc was included in a boxed set of Stone's movies released in January 2001. The R-rated version was finally released in the UK in late 2001 (its postponement necessitated by the Dunblane school massacre in Scotland). The conventional wisdom, among DVD aficionados, however, is that the Region 4 disc is the one to have because it's the only one with an anamorphic transfer, enhanced for widescreen TVs.

Evaluation: *Natural Born Killers* is barely a Tarantino film. Stone, his co-rewriters, his cinematographer, and his editors all turned Tarantino's film into something different: something grander, something more jittery, something more 'important', though there are many more elements from the script than The Mythology would lead you to believe. We now know this because Tarantino's original screenplay is in print, for easy comparison with the film. Tarantino focuses his story on two major chunks, and the story takes place in a much narrower time frame. Wayne Gale's re-creation of Mickey and Mallory's life for a TV show makes up a major middle part, and the prison break is the bulk of the second half. The character Scagnetti is conscripted to escort the duo to an asylum, and that accounts for both his presence and Wayne Gale's at the prison. In the end, as a Stone film it is one of his best – ambitious, sexy, creative, and wrestling with ideas. As a Tarantino film, it is barely on the radar. The husk is Tarantino's. Stone has layered it with a surface business in which he invests his ideas about society.

Still, how could it not help us to understand Tarantino even more? Mickey Knox, like Clarence Worley, is a fantasy figure. They are ordinary fellows who as the movie progresses are imbued with almost supernatural skills of combat and cunning. This may be because they are basically borrowed from the same earlier screenplay (*The Open Road*). Mickey and

Mallory make up an extreme form of Clarence and Alabama. And, like Alabama, Mallory is an adolescent vision of a 'perfect girlfriend,' someone who is a partner in crime as well as in life, who shares your interests like a twin. In the end they are less their own people than performers who undermine the accepted codes of behaviour as enunciated by Goffman. The way society deals with their radical disharmonies is to make them public performers, dancing bears for public consumption.

Curiously, the theme of the urge to violence is more prevalent in Tarantino's version of *True Romance* than in *NBK*: in *True Romance*, violence comes easy to people, and two characters (Floyd and Donowitz) make empty promises of violence that offer pathetic comparisons to Clarence and Alabama's cunning. In the end, *Natural Born Killers* — as a Tarantino film — remains more interesting as a road marker in Tarantino's development, a variation on themes preoccupying him at the time that served as a necessary stage to get to ideas such as *Reservoir Dogs, Jackie Brown* and *Kill Bill. 2/5*

4. Pulp Explosion

Near the end of the original script to *True Romance*, Clarence tells the Richard Donner/Oliver Stone-esque movie producer Lee Donowitz his opinion of Oscar movies.

'You know, most movies that win a lot of Oscars, I can't stand. *Sophie's Choice, Ordinary People, Kramer Vs. Kramer, Gandhi*. All that stuff is safe, generic, coffee-table dog shit. Like that Merchant-Ivory claptrap. All those assholes make are unwatchable movies from unreadable books . . . They ain't plays, they ain't books, they certainly ain't movies. They're films. And do you know what films are? They're for people who don't like movies. *Mad Max*, that's a movie. *The Good, The Bad, And The Ugly*, that's a movie. *Rio Bravo*, that's a movie. *Rumble Fish*, that's a fuckin' movie. And, *Comin' Home In A Body Bag*, that's a movie. It was the first movie with balls to win a lot of Oscars since *The Deer Hunter*.'

On his audio commentary track to *True Romance*, Tarantino admits that Clarence's views reflected his own at the time, but now-Oscar-recipient Tarantino, perhaps mellowed by age and success, has amended this view. Tarantino now thinks the Academy Of Motion Picture Arts And Sciences – the organization that Peter Biskind amusingly calls the 'congress of ancients' – has been doing much better lately.

His own films might be testimony to that impression. *Pulp Fiction*, the hipster hit of 1994, was nominated for no fewer than seven Academy Awards. Though Tarantino and his writing partner Roger Avary were the only ones anointed by the Academy for their work on the film, that in itself was a meager sum of evidence that the Academy was indeed trying to shake off its fuddy-duddy image and get with the times (if, that is, an institution of some 6,000 voting members can be said to be a beast with a single mind).

To film buffs nurturing a love-hate relationship with the Academy, since the 1990s the screenplay Oscar has been the true marker of the year's best picture. Films such as *The Usual Suspects* (1995), *Fargo* (1996), *L. A. Confidential* (1997), and *Gods And Monsters* (1998) comprise something of an internal 'shadow' Oscar that designates true value as opposed to the bloated crowd pleasers that usually receive Best Picture (*Forrest Gump* won the year *Pulp Fiction* was nominated).

Pulp Fiction Facts

In most of 1992 and through much of 1993, Tarantino was promoting *Reservoir Dogs* at international festivals and in the media, and coasting on the unique goodwill the film had created for him in Hollywood. The film geek who didn't have a girlfriend until he was 26 was now, according to The Mythology, a regular Warren Beatty. Temporarily broken up with Grace Lovelace, he was reportedly going out with such women as a British journalist named Karen Krizanovich and actress Emily Lloyd. He revelled in his first appearance on the cover of a magazine (*Orbit*) and met Madonna, who disputed his debut film's thesis about *Like A Virgin* but told him that her favourite scene was the ear slicing ('Torture,' she told him, 'is sexy,' before handing him a copy of her book *Sex*).

But for five months in early 1992, roughly January to May after *Reservoir Dogs'* premiere at Sundance, Tarantino fled to Amsterdam. (Coincidentally, Scorsese once shot part of *Who's That Knocking At My Door?* in that city with Keitel.) There, and partly with the assistance of Avary, he cobbled together the script to *Pulp Fiction*, resurrecting the old idea he had had with Avary for an anthology film and incorporating into it a script he purchased from Avary called *Pandemonium Reigns* (which became 'The Gold Watch' story in the final film). Once upon a time, back in the late 1980s, what became *Pulp Fiction* was going to be an anthology film with Tarantino filming only one of the three or four stories. Avary and Tarantino also ransacked their notes for other scenes and bits of dialogue. The Mia date scene was a story that had been brewing in Tarantino's mind for some time, partially inspired by the situation in *Out Of The Past*. Tarantino wrote the script in his hotel room and in Betty Boop, a hash bar (when he left, he saddled the video rental store Cult Video with a $150 bill).

Meanwhile, Tarantino and Lawrence Bender made a development deal with Danny DeVito's production company, Jersey Films, thanks partially to a friendship with Stacey Sher, whom Tarantino had met in autumn 1991 at a *Terminator 2* screening. Sher helped them secure the rights to the Stealer's Wheel song for *Reservoir Dogs* (and Tarantino also apparently dated Sher for a while). Jersey Films bought the script to *Pulp Fiction* for nearly a million dollars, and in a complex arrangement Tarantino and Bender's company A Band Apart (loosely named after a Godard film) received development money and office space in exchange for Jersey's right to sell the film to a studio. The first studio that Jersey approached was TriStar, to which Jersey Films was obliged to show projects first. TriStar passed on the script for reasons not publicly stated but perhaps having to do with the film's drugs and violence, at which point history was made when Disney, in the form of its newly purchased subsidiary Miramax, stepped in to finance the film. Miramax had apparently enjoyed working with Tarantino on *Reservoir Dogs*, which it distributed, and now having funds to invest in film production, made *Pulp Fiction* its debut project.

Tarantino began assembling a cast. Actors he approached included Michael Madsen (who decided to go with *Wyatt Earp* instead) and Samuel L. Jackson (who got the part over Lawrence Fishburne). Paul Calderon almost got the Jules part but ended up playing the bartender in Wallace's club. Uma Thurman was approached for Mia, but Tarantino at first didn't want her and then made a compete turnaround and decided he favoured her, only to have her waver about doing the film. (Other actresses queried about the role include Meg Ryan, Brigitte Nielsen, Isabella Rossellini, Daryl Hannah, Joan Cusack, Michelle Pfeiffer, and Roseanna Arquette, who ended up playing Jody instead, for which Pam Grier auditioned.) Sylvester Stallone and Matt Dillon were considered for Butch before it was offered to Bruce Willis (who had wanted to play Vincent), then a mega-star who, like all of the major stars in a deal arranged by Bender, worked for the same pay scale but were rewarded with profits from the film's box office. Weinstein apparently advocated Daniel Day-Lewis for the Vincent Vega role, but The Mythology is especially keen about the participation of John Travolta. According to legend, Travolta was startled to realize, when he went to visit Tarantino and discuss the film, that the director was residing in the same apartment the actor had first lived in when he came to Los Angeles. (Cathryn Jaymes' assistant Victoria Lucai – later Tarantino's – had found the apartment for Tarantino.) The two talked, played a couple of board games based on Travolta's shows, and then, late in the evening, Tarantino apparently laid into Travolta for betraying his promise as an actor to his fans. Hurt and moved by Tarantino's concern, Travolta reciprocated by taking the risk of appearing in a drugs and violence movie and giving one of his best performances.

Shooting took place in winter 1993. Portland, Oregon, movie reviewer Dawn Taylor was raised in the same area in which *Pulp Fiction* (and later *Jackie Brown*) was shot. She recalled:

Something interesting about Tarantino to me is the location-specific detail in his L.A. films. He lived and worked in the South Bay – an often-overlooked area south of L.A. but north of Orange County – and, when he made his films, he used that area for locations. He gives a shoutout to the area's uncool/geographically inconvenient status in Pulp Fiction *when Mr. Wolf offers Jules and Vincent a ride home, but when they say they live in Redondo and Inglewood, Wolf says, 'Move outta the sticks, fellas.'*

In Pulp Fiction, *the Hawthorne Grill (where I had a job as a waitress when I was 20, back when it was called Holly's) is on Hawthorne Boulevard, about a mile south of Inglewood. Hawthorne's a major commercial artery through the South Bay – drive another five or so miles further south and you'll find Del Amo Fashion Square, the mall used in* Jackie Brown.

On the back of the Jack Rabbit Slim's menu included in the Pulp Fiction *DVD package, the restaurant's address is given as 1451 Artesia Blvd. – and Artesia's another major street that cuts through Redondo, Hawthorne, and Inglewood.*

The thing that strikes me is that most directors 'cheat' locations – they shoot all over the L.A. area, choose locations based on how the place looks, and then cobble it together regardless of real-life geography – knowing that only the most anal-retentive Los Angeles resident will notice that the mall they're shooting in is really in the Valley, or that the ocean ought to be on the other side of the car if they're driving south from the airport to Marina Del Rey.

But Tarantino is that anal-retentive guy – in Jackie Brown, *the beachfront apartment is in Hermosa Beach (most directors would have made it Santa Monica or Venice), and all the locations are appropriate for that – the Inglewood scenes really are in Inglewood, the Cockatoo Inn really is in Hawthorne, and that's really its bar. The Del Amo mall really is the South Bay's big mall.*

These are details that only someone from L.A. – possibly even only someone from the South Bay – would notice and appreciate.

Pulp Fiction was edited and ready to debut at the Cannes

Film Festival in May 1994. By that time, *True Romance* had appeared, and there was buzz about Oliver Stone's *NBK*. Travolta apparently convinced Harvey Weinstein of Miramax to delay the release of *Pulp Fiction* until autumn, to avoid unnecessary competition with Tarantino's other film as well as to position *Pulp Fiction* as an art house entry that would appeal to youngsters and award-giving bodies. The strategy worked. Having already won the Palme d'Or at Cannes, the film went on to make over $200 million around the world and then garner an Oscar the following spring.

During this time period, *Pulp Fiction* didn't wholly consume Tarantino. The day after an early screening of *Reservoir Dogs*, Tarantino got a call from a director friend named Jeff Burr who asked him to take on a bit part in a film he was doing that also starred cult favourite Bruce Campbell. Tarantino did so, appearing as a hospital orderly in *Eddie Presley*, a low-budget effort about an Elvis impersonator. And Tarantino and Bender took steps to produce Roger Avary's underrated *Killing Zoë*.

Pulp Fiction (1994)

Cast: John Travolta (Vincent Vega), Samuel L. Jackson (Jules Winnfield), Uma Thurman (Mia Wallace), Amanda Plummer (Yolanda/Honey Bunny), Tim Roth (Ringo/Pumpkin), Bruce Willis (Butch Coolidge), Fabienne (Maria de Medeiros), Quentin Tarantino (Jimmie Dimmick), Harvey Keitel (Winston 'The Wolf' Wolfe), Frank Whaley (Brett), Burr Steers (Roger), Ving Rhames (Marsellus Wallace), Rosanna Arquette (Jody), Eric Stoltz (Lance), Steve Buscemi ('Buddy Holly'), Christopher Walken (Captain Koons), Julia Sweeney (Raquel), Lawrence Bender (Long-Hair Yuppie Scum/'Zorro'), Peter Greene (Zed), Stephen Hibbert (The Gimp), Dick Miller (Monster Joe).

Crew: Producers: Lawrence Bender; Executive Producers: Danny DeVito, Michael Shamberg, Stacey Sher; Co-executive Producers: Richard N. Gladstein, Bob Weinstein, Harvey Weinstein; Studio: Miramax; Screenplay: Quentin Tarantino; Story: Roger Avary, Quentin Tarantino; Photography: Andrzej Sekula; Editor: Sally Menke; Production Designer: David Wasco; Costume Designer: Betsy Heimann; Sound Editors: Stephen H. Flick; Casting Director: Ronnie Yeskel, Gary M. Zuckerbrod; Special Effects Co-ordinator: Larry Fioritto; Running time: 154 minutes (168-minute special edition); Ratings: UK, 18; USA, R; HK, III.

Plot: Los Angeles. Present day. In five interwoven and over-lapping stories, a professional enforcer decides to go straight and wander the earth like Caine in *Kung Fu*; a boxer defies a crime boss by not throwing a fight and then ends up trapped with him in the basement of a pawnshop run by two insane Southerners and their chained-up, monstrous relative; another hit man, assigned the task of baby-sitting the crime boss' girl-friend, ends up having to rescue her from a drug overdose; and the two hit men have to clean up the mess from the accidental shooting of a hostage.

Time Banditry: If *Pulp Fiction* is famous for anything, it is the juggling of the narrative's elements. It takes a couple of view-ings, or a visit to GodsAmongDirectors.com, to put the story in the right order. The story actually 'begins' with Vincent and Jules in the car on the way to pick up the suitcase. On the way back to Marcellus' bar, Sally LeRoy's, out near the airport, they accidentally shoot Marvin, their 'inside man' on this job. This leads to the detour to Jimmie's house and the Bonnie situation with Winston Wolf. (One Internet critic has suggested that Jimmie is Wallace's nephew by marriage, while in an interview Tarantino himself asserted that Jimmie used to work for

Wallace.) After they clean up they go to the diner, where Jules announces he is quitting and they encounter Honey Bunny and Pumpkin. They stop at Wallace's club, where they pass by Butch, the fighter ordered to take a dive. Vincent doesn't like Butch (who 'keys' Vincent's car in revenge). Presumably, Jules then quits. Vincent is next seen buying drugs, getting high, and going to Mia's for their night out while Wallace is away on business. They go to a retro diner, win a dance contest, and then return to her place. Vincent emerges from the bathroom to discover that Mia has mistaken his heroine stash for cocaine and overdosed. Vincent drives her back to his pusher's house, where they inject her with adrenalin. They agree that Wallace will be kept in the dark about their adventure. The next night (or perhaps simultaneously the same night) Butch wins the fight he was supposed to throw. He makes his way to the motel where his girlfriend Fabienne is stashed. The next morning he learns that Fabienne has neglected to bring Butch's watch, which once belonged to his father, a Vietnam POW, and the fighter realizes that he must go get it. Marcellus and Vincent have been laying in wait inside Butch's apartment, but Butch happens to arrive when Vincent is in the loo and Marcellus is out getting them coffee (Jules having quit). Butch shoots Vincent and then tries to run down Marcellus on the street. That doesn't work, and they end up prisoners in the basement of a pawnshop owned by two Southerners. Butch manages to free himself and save Marcellus, who vows no harm will come to him if he refuses to speak of these events and stays out of town. Butch drives off on one of the Southerners' motorcycles and picks up his girlfriend. That's the true order. But what is the purpose of the shuffling, besides cost cutting (as in *Reservoir Dogs*) or simple audience attention-grabbing? One of Tarantino's stated structural approaches to scripts is to provide 'answers first, questions later.' It also increases the poignancy level (as we will also see in *Kill Bill*). It's moving at the end when we see Vincent walk off, knowing what we know about his immediate future. Roger Ebert suggests that the film is structured so that each of its parts ends on a moment of redemption.

Violent Moments: As with *Reservoir Dogs*, not as many as you might think: Jules casually shoots the 'Flock of Seagulls' character then shoots Brett. Both Jules and Vincent shoot Bathroom Guy. In the car, Vincent accidentally shoots 'inside man' Marvin (though off-screen). Butch shoots Vincent, and then Butch kills the Gimp and Maynard. Several of the deaths happen outside the narrative: Floyd Wilson, Butch's opponent, for example.

Language: The so-called 'n-word' is uttered 13 times in the film, by Jules and Wallace, the Jimmie character, who uses it three times, and Lance and Maynard, who use it once each. 'Fuck' is spoken 271 times. Yet Tarantino's use of the word proved influential. The comical use of the word (37 times) in the famous and brilliant 'fuck' scene in the fourth episode (*Cold Cases*) of the first season of HBO's *The Wire* is inconceivable without Tarantino's precedence.

Key Quote: Jules: 'Let's get into character.'
Jules: 'The path of the righteous man is beset on all sides with the iniquities of the selfish and the tyranny of evil men. Blessed is he who in the name of charity and goodwill shepherds the weak through the valley of darkness, for he is truly his brother's keeper and the finder of lost children. And I will strike down upon those with great vengeance and with furious anger those who attempt to poison and destroy my brothers. And you will know that my name is the Lord when I lay my vengeance upon thee.'

Codes Of Honour: It bears pointing out that despite the crime milieu of the film, it is for the most part a workaday world, wherein Jules and Vincent perform tasks for their boss, Marcellus, and obey the tenets of that relationship. Within that context, loyalty as the theme of the film inflects most of the action. Honey Bunny and Pumpkin (familiar Tarantinoesque lovers on a crime spree) are loyal to each other. Mia, by contrast, is a wife not above a little flirtation, and Lance's wife, Jody, is an unbearable, pretentious shrew. Boyfriends tend to be loyal romantics: Jules is a vegetarian because his girlfriend is, and Butch indulges his girlfriend's neuroses. Jules and Vincent, the film's only happy couple, are also loyal to each other. But one thing to bear in mind: Vincent isn't a very nice guy. He picks on Butch for no reason (possibly even spurring Butch's decision to disobey Marcellus) and is petulant when Mr. Wolf shows up to bail them out of trouble. Finally, 'keying' another guy's car is viewed as more serious a crime than murder.

The Tarantino Alternate Universe: With *Pulp Fiction*, the Tarantino universe of brand names not only took off but also began to attract attention. Thus, Red Apple cigarettes, Big Kahuna burgers, and Jack Rabbit Slim's, sketched in passing in *Reservoir Dogs*, have a full flowering here, with trademarks and packaging. Jack Rabbit Slim's is apparently also based on Ed Devebic's, at 134 North La Cienega. Tarantino's resistance to product placement is so intense that his staff invented a brand of boxing gloves for the film (Ringside). Butch also eats Sam's Toasted Pastries.

The Music: As pop tunes were to *Reservoir Dogs*, surf music is to *Pulp Fiction*, the signature sound of its landscape. The film begins with a blast of guitar strumming in *Misirlou* performed by Dick Dale And His Del-Tones, a magisterial piece of pop music with Mexican flourishes. Also in the credits is *Jungle*

Boogie by Kool & The Gang (the song switching over at the music supervisor credit). *Son Of A Preacher Man* by Dusty Springfield appears when Vincent arrives at Mia's. Tarantino has said that the scene was unimaginable without that tune and that he would have dropped it if he couldn't get the rights to the song. In Jack Rabbit Slim's, bits are heard of *Lonesome Town* by Ricky Nelson, *Since I First Met You* by The Robins, and *Teenagers In Love* by Woody Thorne. Travolta and Thurman dance to *You Never Can Tell*, written and performed by Chuck Berry. *Bullwinkle Pt. 2* by the Centurians plays in the dreamy back projection sequence of Vincent driving from Lance's to Mia's. Elsewhere in the film come *Strawberry Letter 23* by The Brothers Johnson, *Bustin' Surfboards* by The Tornadoes, *Let's Stay Together* by Al Green, Urge Overkill's version of Neil Diamond's *Girl, You'll Be A Woman Soon*, *If Love Is A Red Dress (Hang Me In Rags)* by Maria McKee (in Maynard's shop), *Flowers On The Wall* by The Statler Brothers (when Butch is driving away from his apartment), and *Out Of Limits* by The Marketts. The movie ends with *Surf Rider* by The Lively Ones.

Magpie Moments: With *Pulp Fiction*, Tarantino's referentiality begins in earnest. There are so many references (both here and in *Kill Bill*) that one little paragraph will fail to do them justice. IMDb.com lists 96 titles alone, from *The Great Train Robbery*, made in 1903, to *Point Of No Return*, from 1993, the year before *Pulp Fiction*. Several of the references are simply movie posters on the wall of Jack Rabbit Slim's, but there are other key references that are antecedents to the film. One is Mario Bava's *Black Sabbath*, a horror anthology film from 1963 that served in part as the inspiration for *Pulp Fiction*. The set-up for Butch's story comes from *The Set-Up* (1949). *Modesty Blaise*, the comic strip by Peter O'Donnell that led to a series of novels and a film adaptation, forms an interesting nexus of references. The novel is Vincent's bathroom reading. But also the book features a killer whose trademark is a biblical rant similar to Jules'. In the film version by Joseph Losey from 1966, Modesty finds a partner in Amsterdam, the same city where Vincent had been living for three years before the chronological beginning of the narrative of *Pulp Fiction*. The rant also has its roots in *The Night Of The Hunter* (1955), *Take A Hard Ride* (1975), and Sonny Chiba's TV series *Shadow Warriors* (1980). Jackson's *Ezekiel* 25:17 rant also has roots in Chiba's *Karate Kiba* (1974). The most complicated influence comes from *Curdled*, a short film from 1991 by Reb Braddock that Tarantino apparently liked so much he helped produce it as a feature (which contains some references to *From Dusk Till Dawn*). Tarantino also cast its star, Angela Jones, as Esmeralda the cab driver. In the film she plays a woman who cleans up crime scenes, not unlike Winston Wolf. Harvey Keitel had a similar role in *Point Of No Return* (1993), the American remake of *La Femme Nikita*, and a little bit of *Psycho* also appears. The credits mimic the font and colourings of the opening title sequence for *Policewomen* (1974). The set for Jack Rabbit Slim's comes from *Speedway* (1968) and Hawks' *Red Line 7000* (1965). Butch telling Zed, 'You want that gun, don't you, Zed? Go ahead and pick it up. I want you to pick it up' comes from *Rio Bravo* (1959). Other references, among many, include *Charley Varrick* (1973), for Marcellus' promise of pain to Zed; *On The Waterfront* (1954), for the name of Butch's opponent; *Kiss Me Deadly* (1955), for the glowing box (along with *Repo Man*, from 1984); *Jules and Jim* (1962), for the names of two characters; Ringo Lam for the name of Pumpkin; *Deliverance* (1972), for Maynard and Zed in a scene that re-creates similar incidents from *American Me* (1992); *The Texas Chainsaw Massacre* (1974), for the saw Butch picks up; *Air Force* (1943), for the name Wynocki, used by Captain Koons; and *American Boy: A Profile Of Steven Prince* (Scorsese's 1978 documentary), for the adrenalin story. When Travolta and Thurman dance they borrow moves from the 1960's *Batman* TV series and *The Aristocats* (1970). The long motel room scene between Butch and Fabienne replicates similar scenes in most of Godard's films. Many titles are just mentioned or alluded to in the dialogue, such as *Even Cowgirls Get The Blues* (1993) and *Urban Cowboy (1980)*, films with Thurman and Travolta respectively, are obliquely cited in dialogue between Vincent and Mia. Jody hovering ecstatically over the adrenaline injection rhymes with a similar image of Jane Greer in a scene in *Out Of The Past*.

Biographical Shoutouts: Tarantino's mother, Connie, and stepfather, Curt, supported the anti-war movement, and Tarantino's interest in Vietnam and in the genre-blending films of Anthony Dawson and Antonio Margheriti speaks to that. Mia's haircut is not only in imitation of Louise Brooks and Anna Karina but was based on the hairstyle of his friend Catalaine Knell, who introduced (or tried to introduce) Tarantino to fetish object and prospective actress Brigitte Nielsen. Tony Scott also borrowed Knell's hairstyle for Nielsen's role in *Beverly Hills Cop II* (1987). Lance is named after Tarantino's old boss Lance Lawson. Lance is a slightly more active version of Floyd from *True Romance*, and both have analogs in real roommates whom Tarantino endured. Big Jerry Cab Company is a shoutout to Tarantino's friend Gerry Martinez, whose brother also painted the picture of Mia in her apartment (based on a portrait of Tarantino's former girlfriend Grace Lovelace). One of the boxing posters announces Vossler versus Martinez, two friends of Tarantino's. As at the start of *Natural Born Killers*, lovers commit a crime in a diner. Butch is taking Fabienne to Knoxville, which is Tarantino's birthplace. Vincent is also driving Tarantino's own 1964 Chevelle Malibu convertible (later stolen). Lance is shown eating one of Tarantino's favourite cereals, the now discontinued Fruit Brute, one of the 'monster' breakfast cereals of the 1970s. Some of the clocks in the film are set at 4:20, 420 supposedly being police code for a marijuana offence, but in fact this is an urban legend. *Pulp Fiction* anticipates *Kill Bill* by having Jules seek to emulate Caine, the character David Carradine played in the cult TV series *Kung Fu*. Mia's waking up suddenly and rabidly was the actress' own contribution, having seen a tiger similarly come out of sedation on the set of *The Adventures of Baron Munchausen* (1988). Tarantino has said that the piercing conversation was something he overheard in a diner. And of course, this is the film in which Fabienne says, 'Any time of day is a good time for pie,' which may come from Video Archives customer Dawn Taylor (see Introduction).

Alternate Versions: There are no truly different versions, except the heavily cut or dubbed TV broadcast editions, but some deleted or longer scenes appear on DVD. Among them is a video interview that Mia conducts with Vincent Vega in her apartment, which makes a wry stab at *sex, lies and videotape*. Among other things she asks Vincent if he's related to folksinger Suzanne Vega (a one-time favourite of Tarantino's) and a series of either-or trivia questions ('*The Brady Bunch* or *The Partridge Family*?'), and she asks if he has ever fantasized being beaten up by a woman (by Diana Rigg as Emma Peel is the answer), and their later diner sequence is longer. Another deleted scene shows Jules fantasizing shooting Pumpkin and Honey Bunny. Also, the conversation between Butch and Esmeralda comes in longer versions, with Butch describing what it feels like to kill a man. Lance tells a story about getting deliberately wrong directions, and in one scene Winston Wolf flirts with the junk-yard owner's daughter. For British television broadcast, the image was reframed to mask needles piercing flesh. In the original script, Vincent shoots Marvin twice in the car.

Foot Notes: The film kicks off with a lengthy debate between Vincent and Jules over the intimacy quotient of a male-to-female foot massage. Uma Thurman is introduced walking before the camera barefoot. On the wall behind Lance in his room are two mismatched disco-era platform shoes mounted on the wall like *objets d'art*. Mia dances barefoot (but so does Vincent). Esmeralda drives her cab barefoot.

Nagging Questions: Why did Vincent leave his gun on the stove when he went to the bathroom? What party is Winston Wolf at in a tuxedo at 8 o'clock in the morning? Why does Fabienne brush her teeth twice? What's in the suitcase? How does Jimmie know Jules? What the hell kind of deal would get Wallace to go into business with college students? Is it a sign that he is slipping?

Critical Reaction: The critics went nuts. The *Washington Post* for example deemed it 'brilliant and brutal, funny and exhilarating, jaw-droppingly cruel and disarmingly sweet.' One of the few pans came from a Palo Alto, California, paper in which the reviewer wrote, 'This fictional world, though rendered imaginatively, can't sustain the movie. The characters undergo no changes whatsoever – which is convenient to this world's amorality,' a statement patently untrue (look at Jules). RottenTomatoes.com gives the film a 94 per cent approval rating.

Release Dates: The film came out in the US on 14 October 1994, followed by a 21 October release in the UK.

Box Office: With a budget of $8 million, *Pulp Fiction* went on to make an astounding $107.9 million in the United States, $212.9 million worldwide.

Awards: BAFTA awards for Supporting Actor (Jackson), Original Screenplay, and Sound; Blue Ribbon award for Best

Foreign Film; Boston Society of Film Critics Awards for Best Film, Director, and Screenplay; Brit Award for Soundtrack; the Cannes Film Festival Palme d'Or; a Casting Society of America award; Chicago Film Critics Association Awards for Best Director and Screenplay; David di Donatello Awards for Best Foreign Actor (Travolta); Edgar Allan Poe Awards for Best Movie; Golden Globe for Screenplay; Independent Spirit Awards for Best Feature, Male Lead (Jackson), Director, and Screenplay; Kinema Junpo Award to Tarantino; London Critics Circle Film Awards for Screenplay and Actor (Travolta); Los Angeles Film Critics Association Awards for Best Picture, Director, Screenplay, and Actor (Travolta); MTV Movie Awards for Best Movie and Best Dance Scene; National Board of Review for Best Movie (in a tie with *Forrest Gump*), and Director; National Society of Film Critics Awards for Best Film, Director, and Screenplay; New York Film Critics Circle Awards for Best Director and Screenplay; Southeastern Film Critics Association Award for Best Movie and Director; Stockholm Film Festival Awards for Best Screenplay, Best Actor (Travolta), and the Bronze Horse; plus 23 various nominations. The biggest award was, of course, the Academy Award for Original Screenplay that went to Tarantino and Avary. Famously, Avary accepted his award and then said he had to go pee, an obvious allusion to *Pulp Fiction*'s major competitor that night, *Forrest Gump* (Gump is shown saying the same thing to JFK when he gets an award). It's too bad Tarantino and Avary fell out. They could have been the Lennon–McCartney of screenwriters.

The DVD: After an initial bare-bones release in May 1998, Miramax released a two-disc set in August 2002, with deleted scenes, a documentary called *Pulp Fiction: The Facts*, an episode of Gene Siskel and Roger Ebert's *At The Movies*, Tarantino's Cannes Film Festival acceptance speech, and a *Charlie Rose*

Show interview, among other things, including an optional text-only commentary track over the film. This set was also released in the UK at the same time.

Evaluation: There are two important points to make about the meaning of *Pulp Fiction*: The first is that, throughout the film, women rule the roost. The other is that all the characters hide things from others.

Pulp Fiction may have begun life as an anthology film (originally called *Black Mask* and making it, in its way, not all that different from *Four Rooms*), but by interlocking its stories the film avoids the perceived stigma of anthology films. The inter-relating of the stories also allows Tarantino the freedom to repeat moments that underscore his themes. For example, the film has three screaming awakenings from sleep, three home invasions (Brett's, Lance's, and Jimmie's, two of them found in bathrobes), and there are three 'deals' in the film, the first between Butch and Marcellus (which Butch breaks), then between Mia and Vincent (to keep their night a secret), and another between Butch and Marcellus. The film is also structured around transitions – from outdoors to indoors, from room to room – and arrivals and departures.

The theme of the film, as Ebert has pointed out, is redemption; Tarantino's transitions and recurrent images are the way he explores that theme. And the viewer can access the core meaning of the movie by asking 'What exactly does Marcellus Wallace do for a living?' Obviously he fixes boxing matches, which means that he is in gambling. But what kind of business would compel him to form an alliance with Brett and his pals? He obviously thought that Brett could sell whatever it is in the suitcase (Avary says that originally it was meant to be jewels, a homophone for the name of the container's courier, Jules). What it most definitely is not is drugs. Marcellus appears to reject drugs (which may be why he lives in the end), while his underling Vincent has returned from Amsterdam a drug addict. Perhaps this is why Mia is so freaked out about her overdose – Marcellus doesn't know that she dabbles in cocaine.

Below Marcellus and his interests is a real pecking order. Jimmie feels that he can be critical of Jules but is subservient when Winston Wolf shows up. Vincent thinks he can have contempt for Butch and resists taking orders from Wolf (one of Vincent's paradoxes is that he complains about rude people but is fairly rude to others).

But the ultimate arbiters of power and hierarchies are the film's women.

Naturally, in a world ruled by women, the men are going to be ambivalent about them. On the one hand, Tarantino can name the Harley after his then-girlfriend Grace but also present women as demandingly neurotic (Fabienne and her trivial worries). It's a view of women similar to the one found in *Bugsy*, such as the scene in which Virginia Hill manipulates Bugsy into letting her go along on what is supposed to be a hit, and then, when he relents, she delays the event further by saying, 'Let me get my things.' Thus, the worst thing that can happen to a man is to be 'made a woman,' as Marcellus is by Zed. After all, as Jules tells Brett, the only person who gets to fuck Marcellus Wallace is Mrs. Wallace. All of this suggests a heretofore-unremarked connection or sympathy between Tarantino and Norman Mailer, novelist and occasional film-maker of male existentialism.

A fascination with tough women, one of Tarantino's fixations, underlies the film. In the cut video interview scene Vincent tells Mia that he has fantasized about being beaten up by Emma Peel of *The Avengers* (coincidentally, in 1998, Uma Thurman played Emma Peel in the movie adaptation of *The Avengers* and then of course went on to play Tarantino's own Peel act-alike, The Bride). The women of *Pulp Fiction* are not immune to violence. Jody looms over Mia during the panic scene. Mia herself leaves a trail of damaged men (Antwan Rocky Horror, defenestrated). Esmeralda the cabbie is sexily interested in what it is like to kill a man.

Set against these *femmes fatales* is male incompetence. One recurring motif is that most of the weapons don't work at a crucial moment (Bathroom Guy's gun), or *do* work, but disastrously (Vincent accidentally killing Marvin). Perhaps this is the point of Vincent reading *Modesty Blaise*. In his own small way he is trying to access the power of women (or continue to turn himself on with images of violent women?).

Once again, another subtext to the film is storytelling and performance, from Vincent's and Lance's stories to each other (cut down for the final film) to Jules 'getting into character' before a confrontation. Here, however, Tarantino likes to show the wires behind his puppets, using various tricks, such as titles and obviously fake backdrops behind cars, that alert the viewer to the falsity of what they are seeing.

Pulp Fiction proves upon repeat viewings to be a deeper, more complex film than has yet been acknowledged by most critical studies. *5/5*

5. Overexposure

When *Pulp Fiction* was released, no one – least of all the director – expected there to follow a three-year hiatus between *Pulp*, released in fall 1994, and Tarantino's next feature, which appeared in December 1997. The hiatus was partially due to Tarantino spending a year promoting the film, adding considerably to its profit, and then taking a year off.

Still, the Tarantino industry was busy, at both ends. On one side of the spectrum, Tarantino was active as an actor, TV director, and script doctor. On the other, several books and scores of articles helped pump up both Tarantino's reputation and The Mythology – until the media decided *not* to like Tarantino, at which point it became difficult to miss the fact that a certain *froideur* had seized the critical community, and maybe even a large segment of the public that pays attention to the caprices of that bitch-goddess, reputation. This disdain overlapped with the release of *Jackie Brown* – but more on that later.

The Tarantino Book Industry

If there were any measure of Tarantino as a cultural force, it would be the publication of no fewer than four biographies and two guidebooks during 1995–96. Many directors don't have even *one* book written about them. These include some of Tarantino's contemporaries, such as Alexandre Rockwell and Allison Anders, but also old-timers such as Cy Endfield who are 'Tarantinoesque.' By contrast, 18 books by or about Scorsese have appeared, and the number of Hitchcock critiques in my collection is currently 82.

The first Tarantino book to hit the shelves was *Quentin Tarantino: The Man And His Movies*, Jami Bernard's bio from HarperCollins. Bernard was at that time a movie reviewer for the *New York Daily News*, had written a few other books on movie trivia and had been nominated for a Pulitzer in 1991 (when she was at the *New York Post*). Bernard manages to come up with quite a sizable amount of information in what must have been a short amount of time and appears to have talked to several of Tarantino's associates and intimates. It is not always clear, however, if quotes come from interviews with her or from other sources: the book lacks an index, a bibliography and endnotes. Bernard's book is *the* source for rotten gossip about the *auteur*. She is sympathetic and intrigued but quotes everybody, giving often-contradictory impressions of Tarantino, sometimes about the same incident. Bernard is best on the then under-researched early years, although careless reading can scramble the onrush of names for Video Archives co-workers and early collaborators. Bernard's book also has a nifty, emotional ending.

Next came Jeff Dawson's *Quentin Tarantino: The Cinema Of Cool*. Dawson was a writer at *Empire* magazine, and his book for the most part has the polished zing of good magazine journalism. Like Bernard's, Dawson's book covers the period up to *Four Rooms*, with the later years 'bulkier' in content than the early ones.

Wensley Clarkson's *Quentin Tarantino: Shooting From The Hip* followed Dawson's book. Clarkson is a prolific writer of books including biographies of Tom Cruise and John Travolta. Clarkson, according to an author's note, also has various screenplays in stages of development and elsewhere lays claim to knowing Tarantino from the fanboy circuit. Like Dawson's book, Clarkson's has the virtue of an index, but unlike all the other quickie bios, this one appears to have had the approval of and unlimited access to Tarantino's mother, who spoke freely while attempting to set the record straight. One consequence is that Clarkson's volume has the best illustrations (for starters there are around 25 early family snapshots) and a few details that the others don't. His chronology is maddeningly difficult to follow, however.

Finally, there was Paul A. Woods' *King Pulp: The Wild World Of Quentin Tarantino*, also going up only to *Four Rooms*. It is at once both the most intellectually rigorous and the slightest of the quartet. Woods redeemed himself four years later, in 2000, by issuing *Quentin Tarantino: The Film Geek Files*, an excellent, must-have anthology of reviews and journalism about Tarantino and his films that serves as kind of a parallel volume to this bio and which contains the best single essay I've yet read on the director, *The Next Best Thing To A Time Machine*, by Peter N. Chumo III. But it should also be pointed out that Woods includes in the middle of his first book a marvellous and revelatory interview with Tarantino on his top-ten list, with a detailed account of his favourite Italian directors. Note also that of these four authors, three are British, which gives a measure of the UK mania over Tarantino.

To the fellow writer struggling with a book about Tarantino, these volumes can be both helpful and frustrating. They ramble, they are repetitious, and they obscure what should be clear. Bernard has someone named Paul Tatagliarone (instead of Paul Calderon) getting Jackson's role in *Pulp*, while Clarkson seems to think that comedian George Carlin is black. Often they disagree on simple facts. For example, is he a Jerry or a Gerry Martinez? Clarkson and Dawson have Jerry; Woods has Gerry. Given that his published author's name is Gerald Martinez, I'm *guessing* that it could be Gerry, but since he is also the recipient of a shoutout in *Pulp Fiction* – Big Jerry Cab Co. – it must be Jerry.

The problem for the collector and the Tarantino fanatic is that all four books are essential. But together they create a reasonable-seeming, rounded portrait. You just can't trust anything that just *one* of them says. For example, Clarkson has the title of Tarantino's first credit both *After Midnight* and *Past Midnight*, attributes a line to Clarence that is really Len's, and has Clarence writing 'You're so cool,' when it is Alabama doing so. But then, all books contain errors – undoubtedly including this one (and if you find any while reading this, please e-mail me at dkholm@mac.com, both in case there is a later, revised version, and because I want to know).

The four bios of Tarantino reached one crucial achievement. They helped to create, or at least solidify, The Mythology, that concatenation of facts, factoids, myths, wishful thinking, and retribution that make up the public life of the director. Such publicity was a remarkable thing to have happened to someone so young and may have seemed just one more thing that appeared to be his due. And despite how embarrassing it might be to have aspects of one's childhood revealed in relentlessly investigatory books – one's eating habits, the sound of one's voice, what one did or didn't do with any given woman – in the end the reality fits right into Tarantino's well-informed plan to establish reputation. He may not have known that books would be written about him so early, or have been able to control the ones that did come out, but they represent a key component of his early reputation.

What's A Tarantino When He's Not Writing And Directing?

Though Tarantino issued no completely personal works during this three-year time off, he remained fairly busy, writing, acting and making sure that his name was in the news. The constituent parts of his career during this period can be broken down like this:

Acting appearances. During this phase of his career, Tarantino occasionally insisted that he was an actor first, and then a writer-director. To that end, he had a small part as a party guest named Sid (after Sid Haig?) in *Sleep With Me* (1994), the yuppie angst comedy made by the Eric Stoltz–Michael Steinberg team (Rory Kelly directed). Here he riffed on Roger Avary's famous interpretation of the gay subtext to Tony Scott's *Top Gun* ('Kelly McGillis, she's heterosexuality. She's saying, "No, no, no, no, no, no, go the normal way, play by the rules, go the normal way." They're saying, "No, go the gay way, be the gay way, go for the gay way," all right?').

He also appeared as a bartender in *Somebody To Love* (also 1994), Alexandre Rockwell's film about actors, starring Rosie Perez and Harvey Keitel. He provided his voice for the short film *The Coriolis Effect* (1994), made by his fellow writer Louis Venosta, who did *Bird On A Wire*, a film that Tarantino seems to esteem.

But his major dramatic turn in this period was for Jack Baran's oblique *Destiny Turns On The Radio* (1995), playing Johnny Destiny, a fate-like character driving a convertible and affecting a cool sartorial style. Tarantino said he liked the screenplay. While he was shooting this film, *Pulp Fiction* broke, and Dawson describes Tarantino on the set at the start of his biography.

In Robert Rodriguez's *Desperado* (1995), Tarantino has a brief if wordy part, telling a joke. And in 1996 he appeared in Spike Lee's *Girl 6* as a sleazy movie director trying to get an auditioning actress to take off her shirt. This communality with a fellow 'independent' filmmaker was shattered after *Jackie Brown* came out.

TV directing. Tarantino, soon to be a buddy of George

Clooney, helmed an episode of *ER* called *Motherhood* in 1994. The episode has one of the doctors delivering her sister's baby on Mother's Day. Though it was already in the script, one of the subplots has a gang member come in with a severed ear. Tarantino was able to cast fave Angela Jones (the cab driver in *Pulp Fiction*) in the show. The episode first aired on 11 May 1995, the penultimate show of the first season.

Script polishing jobs. Tarantino contributed some dialogue to *Crimson Tide*, Tony Scott's misguided submarine movie released in 1995. Tarantino's writerly relationship to Reb Braddock's feature-length version of *Curdled* (1996) is more complicated; see the chapter on *Pulp Fiction* for details.

The festival circuit. Among other promotional activities, Tarantino went to China as a cultural ambassador along with Allison Anders, the Coen brothers, and several others.

TV and talk show appearances. Tarantino befriended Korean-American stand-up comic Margaret Cho and appeared in an episode of her short-lived sitcom *All-American Girl* playing Desmond in a parody of *Pulp Fiction* called *Pulp Sitcom* (it was episode number 18 of the first season and aired on 22 February 1995). He was also the energetic guest host of *Saturday Night Live* on 11 November 1995 and appeared on talk shows *Dennis Miller Live* and *The Howard Stern Show* in January 1998 while promoting the just-released *Jackie Brown*. He also figured in Sarah Kelly's fascinating feature-length documentary *Full Tilt Boogie* (1997), about the making of *From Dusk Till Dawn*, and appeared as another idolater of Samuel Fuller in the excellent documentary about that director, Adam Simon's *The Typewriter, The Rifle And The Movie Camera* (1996). Tarantino also made an appearance on the *American Film Institute Salute To Clint Eastwood* in 1996, paying obeisance to Leone's favourite star.

Rolling Thunder releases. Also in the wake of *Pulp Fiction*'s success, Miramax chief Harvey Weinstein gave the director and film geek licence to pick and choose films for distribution under the new banner of Rolling Thunder (named after the Paul Schrader-scripted film from 1977 about a returning vet who seeks revenge for the murder of his family). Rolling Thunder released two films in 1996. The first was *Chungking Express* from 1994, the first Kar-Wai Wong film to achieve general distribution in the United States. The second was Jack Hill's *Switchblade Sisters*, a girl gang picture from 1975. Hill directed some of Tarantino's favourite blaxploitation films, including *Coffy*, *The Big Doll House*, and *Foxy Brown*. Rolling Thunder later went on to release or re-release several films, including Kitano's *Sonatine*, Fulci's *The Beyond*, and *Curdled* (Miramax closed down Rolling Thunder in 1997).

Major Works

Despite all these distractions, however, two major Tarantino releases appeared in the period between *Pulp Fiction* and *Jackie Brown*.

The first was Tarantino's segment for *Four Rooms*. It was inspired by the New Wave anthology films such as *Boccaccio '70* and *Ro. Go. Pa. G* that were made in the first flush of enthusiasm for French and Italian cinema in the early 1960s, but also bears hints of *Pulp Fiction*'s roots as an anthology film. The source of the idea is already shrouded in mystery and recrimination but seemed to have been conceived by Alexandre Rockwell at a dinner party as he thought out loud about his and his Sundance compadres' attempt to capture some of the spirit of their New Wave predecessors. He told Tarantino about the idea when the director visited Rockwell for two weeks sometime in 1992. Though Rockwell may have been inspired by *Boccaccio '70*, Tarantino might yet again have found inspiration in *Black Sabbath*, as he did making *Pulp Fiction*.

What happened next is that Miramax put together a deal for the film. Tarantino asked fellow Sundance 1992 grad

Allison Anders (whom he dated platonically, after Grace Lovelace). Tarantino also approached Robert Rodriguez, an honorary member of the group (apparently in the early stages of conception, Richard Linklater was also going to do a segment, but it was dropped). According to quotes in Jami Bernard's effusive chronicle of the film's making, the team got along famously and turned out a fine piece of work (the book was written before the film was released).

That's how The Mythology would have it, anyway. Peter Biskind in *Down And Dirty Pictures*, his controversial history of indie films of the 1990s, quotes many of the same people but has them saying different things. While Rodriguez told Bernard that 'We thought we'd hate each other afterwards, but we didn't,' Rockwell told Biskind that he thought at the time, 'This is working with friends? Maybe I won't like these people at the end of this thing.' Anders added that Tarantino's set was bigger than the other three because 'his head demanded a huge set.' Among other things, Weinstein pressured Rockwell to use Alec Baldwin instead of David Proval.

Personally, I find the contrast between contemporaneous promotional remarks and what the same people say years later in a more reflective mood fascinating . . . Both the speakers and the subject of their later ire must find what finally appears in print disquieting.

In any case, Tarantino's segment was originally called *The Thrill Of The Bet* and was finished shortly before Christmas 1994, just as his fame for *Pulp Fiction* was taking off. The whole film was tinkered with throughout winter and then was tested, cut, and finally released the following Christmas.

Meanwhile, Tarantino was starring in *From Dusk Till Dawn*, Robert Rodriguez's vampire tale derived from what was Tarantino's third finished script, originally written in 1991 for the special effects company KNB EFX Group for $1,500. KNB's Robert Kurtzman, who had heard of Tarantino through the scripts of *True Romance* and *Natural Born Killers*, hired the writer to flesh out a 20-page treatment Kurtzman had come up with along with John Esposito. The goal was that Kurtzman would then direct the film and show off KNB's effects prowess.

With typical tortuousness, however, *From Dusk Till Dawn* only came alive in the wake of Tarantino's post-*Pulp* fame. At one point it almost became a *Tales From The Crypt* movie in a series that includes *Bordello Of Blood*. Though production companies had rejected it, Italian investors were interested. But so was Rodriguez, who decided he wanted to make the film as early as September 1992 when Tarantino first described it to him when they met at the Toronto Film Festival. Rodriguez as director, Tarantino as rewriter and star, the investors, and Miramax's horror film branch, Dimension, all came together around a deal that was profitable for director and star-writer. The $17 million movie was shot in autumn 1995 and released in early 1996.

The Man From Hollywood from Four Rooms (1995)

Cast: Tim Roth (Ted the Bellhop), Bruce Willis (Leo), Quentin Tarantino (Chester Rush), Paul Calderon (Norman), Jennifer Beals (Angela from room 404).

Crew: Producers: Lawrence Bender; Co-producers: Paul Hellerman, Scott Lambert, Heidi Vogel; Executive Producers: Alexandre Rockwell, Quentin Tarantino; Distributor: Miramax; Screenplay: Quentin Tarantino; Story: adapted from *The Man From The South*, from *Alfred Hitchcock Presents*; Photography: Andrzej Sekula; Steadicam Operator: Bob Gorelick; Editor: Sally Menke; Music: original music by Combustible Edison, with non-original music by Juan García Esquivel; Production Designer: Gary Frutkoff; Costume Designer: Mary Claire Hannan; Sound Editor: Bruce Fortune;

Casting Director: Russell Gray; Special Effects: KNB EFX Group; Running time: 23 minutes (98 minutes for whole movie); Ratings: UK, 18; USA, R.

Plot: Los Angeles. New Year's Eve. 6 o'clock in the morning. The Mon Signor Hotel. A crass movie star named Chester Rush, star of *The Wacky Detective* and *The Dog Catcher*, engages in an elaborate bet with one of his factotums, Norman, to replicate a wager from an old episode of *Alfred Hitchcock Presents*, in which a travelling rogue bets a guy desperate for money that he can't light his lighter ten times in a row. Ted, the bellhop, whose first night on the job this is, is enlisted first to bring up the heavy materials (hatches, cutting board) but also to hold the blade and chop off Norman's little finger without hesitation, as a neutral observer. While Chester's manager Leo, and Angela, a resident in one of the other rooms, looks on, Norman and Chester settle down to enact the bet. The lighter fails to ignite with the first attempt, Ted severs the finger, scoops up the money, and leaves.

Time Banditry: *The Man From Hollywood* is told in real time: see the chapter on *Reservoir Dogs*.

Violent Moments: As often happens in a Tarantino movie, the frantic surface of the work makes the viewer think that it's more violent than it really is – although a guy getting his finger chopped off is pretty violent. (In the original TV episode, the finger is spared.)

Language: There are a lot of 'fucks', 193 of them according to the Internet Movie Database.

Key Quote: Chester: 'This is Cristal! Everything else is just piss.'

Codes Of Honour: If anything, *The Man From Hollywood* shows the flip side of Tarantino's code of loyalty. Here, Rush is surrounded by a pair of kowtowing yes men, so servile they are willing to risk their digits. Still, a bet has been made and it must be honoured.

The Tarantino Alternate Universe: A pack of Red Apple smokes is seen near the switchboard in one of the connecting scenes. Chester and his Chevelle appear on the cover of *Hot Car* magazine.

The Music: At the insistence of Anders, the music consists of an original score by Combustible Edison. The group offers up a jaunty, 'comic' score of modernist cocktail music.

Magpie Moments: *The Man From The South*, by Roald Dahl, aired 3 January 1960 and was directed by Hitchcock regular Norman Lloyd from a teleplay by William Fay. It starred Steve McQueen, Peter Lorre, and Katherine Squire. For some reason, the characters in Tarantino's short call the episode *The Man From Rio*. Dialogue citations are made to *Quadrophenia* and Jerry Lewis' comedy *The Bellboy* (1960). At one point the boys cry out, 'Always be closing', a quote from *Glengarry Glen Ross*. Norman's pinky finger is sort of a stand-in for *Reservoir Dogs'* ear. *Four Rooms* opens with a sequence probably directed by Tarantino in which an older bellhop (Marc Lawrence) passes the reins on to Ted. Lawrence is a revered B movie actor who was prolific in the 1930s and later notable for *This Gun For Hire*, *The Asphalt Jungle*, *Dillinger*, and *Key Largo*.

Biographical Shoutouts: The whole story is in a way a variation on what Tarantino's real life might have been like at the time, or what people may have thought he was going through: booze, women, sycophants, bullying of servants, and so forth, the whole parody of Hollywood high life. It's interesting that Tarantino casts himself as an actor rather than a director, and if you didn't know the nature of the relationships, you might think that Rush is the personal manager and Leo the actor. Also the 1964 Chevelle Malibu convertible being wagered (shown on the cover of a magazine) is Tarantino's own car, also used in *Pulp Fiction*.

Alternate Versions: None, though the film was cut severely after previews (though apparently not Tarantino's segment).

Foot Notes: The only digits acknowledged in the film are fingers, but Angela is barefoot, having just bathed.

Nagging Questions: How did Angela end up in Chester's room (there is a passing reference to a swimming pool)? Why do they call the *Alfred Hitchcock* episode by a different title?

Critical Reaction: Low. The film has a 29 per cent Rotten rating at RottenTomatoes.com. Janet Maslin in the *New York Times* called it a 'career-denting fiasco', and Roger Ebert called Tarantino's segment 'disposable'.

Release Dates: 25 December 1995 in the US, and the next day in the UK.

Box Office: With a budget of $4 million, *Four Rooms* went on to make a mere $4.3 million, though the producers insist that it eventually turned a profit.

Awards: *Four Rooms* won a Razzie (the anti-Oscars) for Madonna's performance, and one MTV nomination.

The DVD: Miramax Home Entertainment released a DVD

in April 1999, not enhanced for wide-screen televisions and with no extras. A Region 2 German disc was also released.

Evaluation: There are people who love this segment from *Four Rooms* and people who hate it. It is modestly consistent in its own way with Tarantino's themes but shows the excessive public TV-talk-show side of the director rather than the cunning master of cool. Though the long takes are for the most part handled beautifully, the acting is uneven, and relationships between characters are unclear. And, quite frankly, Tim Roth (miscast after Steve Buscemi declined the project) is horrible, as he is throughout the other segments. His overdone organ grinder's monkey performance is at odds with all the cast members in the rest of the film. Still, the film bears some thematic interest. Just as Mia really wants to win that dance contest, Chester really wants to go through with the bet. Chester, an actor, makes his living as a performer, and, in the Goffmanian sense, he also rules his entourage through a series of small, irrational disruptions, teasings, and challenges. *2/5*

From Dusk Till Dawn (1996)

Cast: Harvey Keitel (Jacob Fuller), George Clooney (Seth Gecko), Quentin Tarantino (Richard Gecko), Juliette Lewis (Kate Fuller), Ernest Liu (Scott Fuller), Salma Hayek (Santanico Pandemonium), Cheech Marin (Border Guard, Chet Pussy, Carlos), Danny Trejo (Razor Charlie), Tom Savini (Sex Machine), Fred Williamson (Frost), Michael Parks (Texas Ranger Earl McGraw), Brenda Hillhouse (Hostage Gloria), John Saxon (FBI Agent Stanley Chase), Marc Lawrence (Old-Timer Motel Owner), Kelly Preston (Newscaster Kelly Houge), Aimee Graham (Blonde Hostage), Heidi McNeal (Red-headed Hostage), Lawrence Bender (Man in diner, uncredited).

Crew: Director: Robert Rodriguez; Producers: Gianni Nunnari, Meir Teper; Co-producers: Elizabeth Avellan, John Esposito, Paul Hellerman, Robert Kurtzman; Executive Producers: Lawrence Bender, Robert Rodriguez, Quentin Tarantino; Distributor: Dimension/Miramax; Screenplay: Quentin Tarantino; Story: Robert Kurtzman; Photography: Guillermo Navarro; Editor: Robert Rodriguez; Original Music: Graeme Revell; Production Designer: Cecilia Montiel; Costume Designer: Graciela Mazón; Sound Editors: Dean Beville; Casting Directors: Elaine J. Huzzar, Johanna Ray; Special Effects Co-ordinator: Thomas L. Bellissimo; Running time: 108 minutes; Ratings: UK, 18; USA, R; HK, III.

Plot: Barstow, California. Present day. A convenience store. A Texas Ranger is bantering with the clerk unaware that the brothers Seth and Richie Gecko happen to be there, too, on their way to Mexico after Richie has busted Seth out of prison and they have robbed a bank. The intruding Ranger falls victim to Richie's irrationality. At a motel, Seth and Richie hide out with Gloria, a hostage from the bank job, but when Seth's back is turned, the psychotic Richie rapes and kills Gloria. Needing a means to make their rendezvous in Mexico, the Geckos hijack the recreational vehicle of the troubled vacationing Fuller family. Jacob Fuller is a minister who doubts his faith in the wake of his wife's death. With him are daughter Kate and adopted son Scott, who is Chinese. Hidden in the Fuller's Winnebago, the pair make a tense crossing into Mexico before the Gecko's take them to the meeting ground, a combination biker bar and strip club called The Titty Twister in an isolated part of the country. Inside the frightening club, the Geckos and the Fullers watch the stage show, which features the dancer Santanico Pandemonium. She teases Richie and after her dance, trouble starts. When Santanico smells blood from Richie's gunshot wound, she leaps upon the man, biting the wound, killing him, and drinking the blood. It turns out that the Titty Twister is the haven of demonic vampires who lure the loner dregs of society to their deaths. For the rest of the night, Seth, the Fullers, and an ever-diminishing gang of bikers must fight off an unyielding hoard of vampires. At dawn, only Seth and Kate remain and drive off on their separate ways, not noticing that the Titty Twister was erected near Aztec ruins.

Time Banditry: *From Dusk Till Dawn* unspools chronologically, but it has a lot of backstory. Some of the things we *don't* see are Seth's breakout, the bank robbery, and Jacob's backstory about his wife's death.

Violent Moments: After the opening shootings and the blowing up of the convenience store, there is no violent action until the final 40 minutes, which takes place in the club and is an orgy of bites, exploding vampire-demons, gunshot wounds, and sunlight-induced vampire incineration.

Language: It's a reasonably foul-mouthed R-rated movie.

Key Quote: Seth: 'Whew! Those acts of God really stick it in and break it off, don't they?'

Codes Of Honour: Seth's loyalty to his insane, hallucinogenic brother Richie is the root code at the heart of *FDTD*. As in *The Godfather*, loyalty to family comes first. Jacob, in turn, is loyal to his family but angry with God, who has taken away his wife in an especially cruel and painful way.

The Tarantino Alternate Universe: Seth comes back to the motel with some Kahuna Burgers, there's a pack of Red Apple cigarettes in Seth's Cougar, and Seth quotes Joe Cabot when he says to Jacob, 'Okay, ramblers, let's get rambling.'

The Music: Among the tunes used in this bluesy score derived from the catalogue are *Dark Night* by The Blasters, *Torquay* by The Leftovers, *Foolish Heart* by The Mavericks, two songs from Stevie Ray Vaughn (*Mary Had A Little Lamb* by Buddy Guy and *Willie The Pimp (And His Cadillac Coffin)* by Bill Carrier and Ruth Elliott Ellsworth), three songs by Tito and Tarantula, and two songs from ZZ Top.

Magpie Moments: *The Desperate Hours* (1955) is the king among many hostage movies and was later remade with Mickey Rourke (1990). *Ring Of Fire* (1961) is one of several road films with hostages. *Vamp* (1986) was the first of the great vampire club movies. *FDTD*'s clutch of surrounded fighters is in the tradition of *Assault On Precinct 13* (1976), with some of that film's dialogue also being quoted. Before Oliver Stone made *NBK*, he was one of Tarantino's favourite writer-directors; thus *Wall Street* (1987) may have created the source for the Geckos' reptilian last name. The Fullers are named after Samuel Fuller. The street outside the Titty Twister is named after the song in *Rio Bravo. The Wild Bunch* (1969) is quoted in the dialogue (the 'What's in Mexico?' Q&A), and the flight to Mexico as a narrative spur comes from *The Getaway* (1972), and in Jim Thompson's novel El Rey is also the destination. Salma Hayek's name comes from the prolific Gilberto Martínez Solares' film *Satánico Pandemonium* (1975), though it is unclear if Tarantino has seen it. (A 1970s L.A. horror movie show host used the same introduction.) Other citations include *Charley Varrick* (1973), *Taxi Driver* (1976), *Bad Taste* (1987), *The Killer* (1989), and *Hot Shots! Part Deux* (1993).

The film anticipates *Kill Bill, Vol. 1* and *Vol. 2* by using Michael Parks (twice) and having a setting in Barstow, California. The use of 'Simon Says' as in *Die Hard With A Vengeance* is probably just a coincidence, since they were made so close together, but the film does anticipate the preacher from *Signs* who loses his faith after his wife dies in a car wreck.

Biographical Shoutouts: The most personal element of the script is the role of Scott as adoptive son to Jacob, just as Tarantino had a succession of step-dads. But also various themes and situations are common to other Tarantino films. There's the talk in the diner, in this case religious talk, as in *Pulp Fiction*; and there's the newscaster describing the criminals' hijinks from *NBK*. Coming home with fast food is echoed in *True Romance*, as is the name Richie; the hostage in a trunk is a trademark shot; and of course the Gecko boys replicate Vince and Vic Vega from *Reservoir Dogs* and *Pulp Fiction*: one's nuts, the other isn't. The pair committing in-tandem shootings resembles *Pulp Fiction* but probably really comes from *Lethal Weapon* or an as-yet unnamed Hong Kong film. Gloria the hostage is played by Brenda Hillhouse, Tarantino's old acting coach. The nice travelling shot of Richie walking to the RV anticipates a similar shot of Michael Madsen approaching his strip bar in *KB, Vol. 2*. Cunnilingus as a theme also comes from *True Romance* and most other Tarantino films.

Alternate Versions: A few moments of deleted vampire violence appear on the DVD, but the film as it stands now is the only version, though in the original screenplay all the Geckos and Fullers survived. However, Tarantino executive produced two excellent sequels that offer intriguing variations on the parent film. Tarantino's pal, the visually imaginative Scott Spiegel, directed *From Dusk Till Dawn 2: Texas Blood Money* (1999). In a deviation from the first film, it features a bank robber bitten by a bat near the ruins of the Titty Twister and then goes on to infect his crew, all under siege by the cops in a bank job gone awry. P.J. Pesce directs *From Dusk Till Dawn*

3: The Hangman's Daughter (2000). Cleverly, it tells the back-story of how Santanico Pandemonium came to rule over the Titty Twister, and incidentally also solves the mystery of what happened to writer Ambrose Bierce (Michael Parks) – the film's subtitle comes from Bierce. Pesce borrows Bierce's theme of the interrupted hanging or death and weaves it throughout the narrative. In key ways it may be the best of the three. Both films were shot in South Africa and went straight to video.

Foot Notes: Richie sees and hesitates over Kate's foot when he drops the RV keys in the motel room. Richie also observes her feet later while in the RV. Santanico Pandemonium (whose toes get sucked by Richie) has a nifty, sexy speech while looming over Seth that Hayek delivers beautifully and is worth quoting in full: 'I'm not gonna drain you completely. You're gonna turn for me. You'll be my slave. You'll live for me. You'll eat bugs because I order it. Because I don't think you're worthy of human blood, you'll feed on the blood of stray dogs. You'll be my footstool. And at my command, you'll lick the dog shit from my boot heel. Since you'll be my dog, your new name will be "Spot". Welcome to slavery.' Clooney's improvised retort, too, is hilarious.

Nagging Questions: Are the monsters vampires or demons? What is the significance of the Aztec pyramid near the club?

Critical Reaction: Reviewers appeared to be divided on this film. Some called it 'great fun', others 'over the top' and 'campy.' At RottenTomatoes.com, the film comes just under the wire for a Rotten rating.

Release Dates: 19 January 1996, in the US, and 31 May 1996 in the UK.

Box Office: With a budget of $17 million, *From Dusk Till Dawn* went on to make $19 million in the United States and $59.2 million worldwide.

Awards: The film won Saturn Awards for Best Horror Film and for Best Actor (George Clooney) from the Academy of Science Fiction, Fantasy and Horror Films; a Silver Scream Award from the Amsterdam Fantastic Film Festival went to Robert Rodriguez; George Clooney won Best Breakthrough Performance from the MTV Movie Awards; and Tarantino was rewarded for his appearance in the film with a Razzie Awards nomination.

The DVD: In October 2000 Miramax released a two-disc special edition with loads of extras, including a yak track (from the laser disc), deleted scenes and various 'making of' shorts. Also included was Kelly's feature-length doc *Full Tilt Boogie*. It should be pointed out that in the American two-disc set the labels are mixed up, so that the movie has the label for the documentary, and vice versa. A version of the film shorter by five minutes was released on disc in the UK in November 1998, followed in September 2001 by a Region 2 pressing of the American two-disc set, but, unlike its American cousin, it's enhanced for wide-screen TVs.

Evaluation: The critics seem not to have 'gotten' *From Dusk Till Dawn*. If viewed in the right spirit, it's great fun. But at the same time the film has some thematic connection to Tarantino's earlier films: the trials created by loyalty, familial and otherwise, the nature of sanity, and the tests brought to bear on faith (as a young teen, Tarantino had a phase as a religious nut). Understandably muted because realized by a different person, the themes are nonetheless present. For example, three of the most interesting moments play with these elements: Jacob's poignant speech to Kate about faith in the diner; later, Seth's rousing theological argument with him during the siege; and then, finally, the painful choices that Seth faces when his own brother has turned. Even more interesting, the two sequels themselves are highly creditable works of action-horror filmmaking.

If nothing else, Tarantino wants you to have fun at the movies. So does Rodriguez. And Tarantino wants to replicate the look and feel and content of the drive-in-style films he loved growing up in the 1970s (the title refers to an audience inducement posted on drive-in marquees). In that regard the director he resembles most is Spielberg, who also is always hunting the Holy Grail of the movies and effects he enjoyed as a kid, and who also, to that end, does a lot of producing. If for nothing else, Tarantino should be lauded for trying to bring back deep pleasure as a standard by which to make and evaluate movies.

When made up as a vampire, by the way, Tarantino looks like Rondo Hatton. 4/5

6. The Wilderness Years

Back in 1978, Quentin Tarantino attempted to steal a mass-market paperback from a grocery store down the street from where he lived. He was caught. His mother grounded him for the rest of the summer. He went in the next week and bought the book. It was a novel by Elmore Leonard called *The Switch*.

Fourteen years later he made a movie based on a Leonard novel that featured the same two criminal characters that appeared in that book.

Rum Punch was published in 1992, but Tarantino saw a prepublication copy of the book and got excited about it. Unfortunately, at the time he couldn't make a commitment to the book as a project. Later, Miramax acquired the rights to it and three other Leonard novels (*Killshot, Bandits,* and *Freaky Deaky*). Miramax also bought the rights to Modesty Blaise books, hoping that he would make a movie based on them starring Uma Thurman (in *Kill Bill,* he may have done a variation of that idea). At that time, Miramax may have bought him Wittgenstein's *Tractatus* if he'd asked for it.

The crazy success of *Pulp Fiction* changed a lot of things. It changed the definition of an 'indie' film. It established Miramax as a power, a real player in Hollywood. It changed the way we view B-movie actors whose time had passed. And it changed Tarantino.

Or he changed himself. Reputedly, the former geek who lived on Denny's took up a more healthful diet. He began training with a boxer. He also fired his longtime manager, Cathryn Jaymes (she said, 'Quentin is Quentin'; he called her a drama queen), signing up with the William Morris Agency (many *Pulp Fiction* cast members were Morris clients). Tarantino also moved from his apartment on Crescent Heights to a large home in the Hollywood Hills near Universal Studios. He was an Oscar-winning screenwriter and as a director was honoured, along with John Woo, Robert Rodriguez, and Kevin Smith at a web site called Gods Among Directors. He began dating Mira Sorvino, winner of a best supporting actress Oscar for *Mighty Aphrodite*.

After *Pulp Fiction, Four Rooms*, and *From Dusk Till Dawn* he worked on several projects. He helped to get Reb Braddock's short film *Curdled* turned into a feature, which was released in 1996.

Then he disappeared (and, as we shall see, not for the last time). Among other things, Tarantino was writing the script to *Jackie Brown*, which he says took a full year. Though he almost gave the book to someone else to shoot, at the last minute Tarantino decided that this was what he wanted for his next film, taking inspiration from, among other movies, the Walter Hill-scripted *Hickey And Boggs* (1972), Bogdanovich's underrated *They All Laughed* (1981), *Straight Time* (1978), from Edward Bunker's novel, and De Palma's *Carlito's Way* (1993). After a lengthy casting period (Sylvester Stallone was interested in playing Louis, John Travolta was considered for Ray Nicolet, and for Max Cherry Tarantino looked at Paul Newman, Gene Hackman, and John Saxon), shooting took place during the winter of 1996–97 and the film was ready for release – and the big publicity push – in December 1997.

Jackie Brown (1997)

Cast: Pam Grier (Jackie Brown), Samuel L. Jackson (Ordell
Robbie); Robert Forster (Max Cherry); Bridget Fonda
(Melanie Ralston); Michael Keaton (Ray Nicolet); Robert De
Niro (Louis Gara); Michael Bowen (Mark Dargus); Chris
Tucker (Beaumont Livingston); Lisa Gay Hamilton
(Sheronda); Tommy 'Tiny' Lister Jr. (Winston); Hattie Winston
(Simone); Sid Haig (Judge); Aimee Graham (Amy, Billingsley
Salesgirl); Laura Lovelace (Steakhouse Waitress); Julia Ervin,
Juliet Long, Michelle Berube, Gillian Iliana-Waters, Christine
Lydon, M.D. (Chicks Who Love Guns); Denise Crosby
(Public Defender); Quentin Tarantino (answering machine
voice).

Crew: Producer: Lawrence Bender; Co-producers: Paul
Hellerman, Elmore Leonard; Executive Producers: Richard N.
Gladstein, Bob Weinstein, Harvey Weinstein; Distributor:
Miramax; Screenplay: Quentin Tarantino, from the novel *Rum
Punch* by Elmore Leonard; Photography: Guillermo Navarro;
Editor: Sally Menke; Original Music: Joseph Julián González;
Production Designer: David Wasco; Costume Designer: Mary
Claire Hannan; Sound Editor: Stephen H. Flick; Casting
Director: Jaki Brown, Robyn M. Mitchell; Special Effects Co-
ordinator: Thomas L. Bellissimo; Special Credits: 'Mighty
Mighty Afrodite Production,' early theatrical versions only; to
Bert D'Angelo's daughter, 'Samuel Fuller – Thanks For
Everything'; Running time: 151 minutes; Ratings: UK, 15 (18
for the DVD); USA, R; HK, IIB.

Plot: Los Angeles. Present day. Jackie Brown, stewardess for a
minor airline, is picked up bringing $50,000 into the country.
She is doing so at the behest of a gun dealer named Ordell. The
ATF wants Ordell, as do the police, who suspect him of

shooting an associate on the verge of flipping on Ordell. Max Cherry, the bail bondsman whom Ordell has hired for both employees, falls for Jackie and watches as she puts together a clever plan to not only avoid termination by Ordell but keep his money and get out of the clutches of the legal system. To that end she presents herself to the ATF as a person who can help them get Ordell. She then convinces Ordell to import $500,000, part of which he might need to finance her silence. During an elaborate money transfer in a mall, under the watchful eyes of the ATF, Ordell's ex-prison buddy Louis and Max, Jackie manages to hand off an empty sack to Ordell's girlfriend, Melanie, and get the real money to Max. Outside the mall, Louis, irritated by Melanie, shoots and kills her. When he meets up with Ordell, they are both surprised that there is no money. Ordell kills Louis. With his world tumbling down around him, Ordell agrees to meet Jackie at Max's office. However, when he arrives, ATF agent Ray Nicolet emerges from hiding and shoots him. Later, Jackie stops by Max's office. She tempts Max with an invitation to go with her out of the country, but he declines. With mixed emotions, he watches her drive away.

Time Banditry: Those observers who suggested that Tarantino was influenced by Kubrick's *The Killing* when making *Reservoir Dogs* were wrong about that connection, but would have been right if they later made it about *Jackie Brown*. During the second money hand off in the shopping mall, Tarantino stops the film, backs up, and takes the viewer through the events once again but from other characters' perspectives. First it's Jackie, then Melanie and Louis, and finally Max. With each stage in the progression, the viewer learns a little more about Jackie's scheme – and about the characters involved in it, willingly or not.

Violent Moments: Most of the violence in *Jackie Brown* occurs just off camera, in shadows, or from a distance (there is a lot more violence in the source book). That includes Ordell's execution of Beaumont in the trunk of a stolen car, Louis' irritated elimination of Melanie in the mall's parking lot, and Ray Nicolet's gunning down of Ordell in Max's office. This discretion is at odds with Tarantino's reputation, but an alert viewing of his previous directorial efforts shows a similar unwillingness to wallow in violence for its own sake.

Language: Just as *Reservoir Dogs* attracted a real or manufactured controversy about its violence, carried over into *Pulp Fiction*, *Jackie Brown* generated a mixed reaction over Tarantino's use of the word 'nigger' (or occasionally, 'niggah'). Spike Lee in particular started a feud with Tarantino over the use of the word, which is primarily spoken by Samuel L. Jackson in the film.

Key Quote: Jackie Brown: 'Well, I've flown seven million miles. And I've been waiting on people almost 20 years. The best job I could get after my bust was Cabo Air, which is the worst job you can get in this industry. I make about $16,000, with retirement benefits that ain't worth a damn. And now with this arrest hanging over my head, I'm scared. If I lose my job I gotta start all over again, but I got nothing to start over with. I'll be stuck with whatever I can get. And that shit is scarier than Ordell.'

Codes Of Honour: If previous Tarantino movies investigated honour, this one shows honour among thieves, which breaks down rapidly. Almost everyone in the film, except for Max Cherry, betrays someone, and Cherry himself 'betrays' his code of ethics, though without consequence. What's also interesting is that frequently the members of this motley gang usually *know* when someone is conspiring against them (Ordell knows that Melanie is scheming), and that very knowledge is something of a reassurance.

The Tarantino Alternate Universe: Manufactured brand names are at a minimum in *Jackie Brown*. There is Teriyaki Donut, in the food court of the mall, which also exists in *Pulp Fiction*. And the shop Busta Cap is invented. Billingsley, the clothing store setting for the handoff is either real and unfindable, out of business, or made up, maybe named after Barbara Billingsley, the mother in *Leave It To Beaver*. A call to the Del Amo mall unearthed no Billingsley.

The Music: Soul music is the soul of *Jackie Brown*. Though *Jackie Brown* isn't really a blaxploitation film, it takes its cues from the spirit of those films from the late 1960s through the 1970s and uses music from the soundtrack of three of them. The film opens with Bobby Womack singing *Across 110th Street*, the theme song of another film starring Anthony Quinn, and proceeds to *Strawberry Letter 23* by The Brothers Johnson, *Baby Love* by The Supremes, *Tennessee Stud* by Johnny Cash, *Inside My Love* by Minnie Riperton, *(Holy Matrimony) Letter To The Firm* by Foxy Brown, *Who Is He (And What Is He To You?)* by Bill Withers, *Cissy Strut* by The Meters, *Monte Carlo Nights* by Elliot Easton's Tiki Gods; *She Puts Me In The Mood* by Elvin Bishop, *Street Life* by Randy Crawford, three pieces by Ron Ayers (*Aragon, Vittrone's Theme – King Is Dead*, and *Escape*), *The Lions And The Cucumber* by The Vampire Sound Incorporation from the soundtrack to *Vampyros Lesbos – The Sexadelic Dance Party*, *Grazing In The Grass* by Orchestra Harlow, *Mad Dog (Feroce)* by Umberto Smaila, *Jizz Da Pitt* performed by Slash's Snakepit, and *La La Means I Love You*, performed by The Delfonics, becomes Max and Jackie's song. *Undun* by The Guess Who and *Midnight Confessions* by The

Grass Roots tell you just about everything you need to know about Melanie. Even a Pam Grier song is included in the mix (*Long Time Woman* when her character is led into detention). *Chicks Who Love Guns* is the original music by Joseph Julian Gonzalez for the video within the film.

Magpie Moments: Unlike Tarantino's previous films and the ones yet to come, *Jackie Brown* is much less tied up with other, similar films, possibly because the source novel is not so involved in cinematic references. However, Jackie Brown is also the name of a (male) character in *The Friends Of Eddie Coyle*. Melanie is shown watching *The Human Beast* (*La Belva Col Mitra*), the last film by uncompromising writer-director Sergio Grieco, made in 1977. Max buying a Delfonics CD replicates a similar scene in *Taxi Driver*. At one point Tarantino quotes from a film by his buddy Tony Scott, *The Fan* (1996), where De Niro, there as here, uses the phrase 'serious as a heart attack.' John Woo's *The Killer* and Cheech and Chong are mentioned in dialogue. Any movie with Pam Grier (*The Big Doll House*, *Coffy*, *Foxy Brown*) is important to *Jackie Brown*, if only through Sid Haig, who is cited and makes an appearance (as a judge). With its setting in the worlds of gun dealing and skip tracing the film evokes *The Friends Of Eddie Coyle* (1973) and *The Hunter* (1980). Most of the film citations appear to be to Tarantino's own movies. Ordell chides Max for not washing his hands, as he does to Vincent in *Pulp Fiction*. Ordell says, 'He didn't have a pot to piss in or a window to throw it out,' which Dick Ritchie says in *True Romance*. Jackie and Butch both drive a white Honda. The black Jones New York pantsuit that Jackie buys is the same one Mia Wallace wears in *Pulp Fiction*, that Elle Driver later wears in *Kill Bill*, and that Chester Rush seems to wear in *The Man From Hollywood*. All of them could be derived from the suit that Isabelle Adjani wears in Walter Hill's *The Driver* (1978). Ordell's hair makes him look like the

Crypt Keeper in the movies and shows derived from the old E.C. horror comics. Jackie closing the door on Ordell and then immediately opening it for Max evokes Fabienne brushing her teeth twice as a time compressor in *Pulp Fiction*. One reference in the book that doesn't appear in the movie is to *Ruthless People*. Leonard has Louis and Ordell complain that the (unnamed) movie stole its plot from their adventure in *The Switch*, wherein they kidnap a millionaire's wife only to discover he doesn't want her back. *Jackie Brown* even makes a reference to *Jackie Brown*: the music the audience hears as Max exits the cinema is the end music for *Jackie Brown*.

Biographical Shoutouts: Tarantino's mother had an African-American best friend and sometime roommate named Jackie Watts. Much of the film was shot in the areas where Tarantino grew up. Melanie is shown watching *Dirty Mary, Crazy Larry* (1974) on TV, a film that starred Fonda's father, Peter Fonda. Melanie's character is in the tradition of irritating wives or girlfriends who appear throughout Tarantino's work, like Jody in *Pulp Fiction*. Max is shown reading a Len Deighton novel while waiting for Jackie: it's part of the *Game-Set-Match* trilogy that Tarantino at one time hoped to film. Tarantino has said that growing up he hated surfers and surfer culture. Did he also hate surfer girls, hence the Jody-like nature of her character? Ordell likes to wear gloves, not unlike O.J. Simpson, and catches Max coming out of the bathroom without washing his hands, reminding us of a theme of *Pulp Fiction*. Ordell's description of cops barging in on him may owe something to Tarantino's own arrest for parking fines.

Alternate Versions: *Jackie Brown* is a lengthy film, and at one time it was even longer. The eventual DVD included several deleted or extended sequences, such as one with Jackie and Sheronda in the mall's food court, Jackie and Ray in the restaurant, Louis and Ordell walking into a bar, and a scene in which Jackie ponders with Max how to set up Ordell. Some scenes appear in the script that were either cut or changed somewhere along the way, such as a conversation between Max and a fugitive he is taking to jail before he picks up Jackie for the first time, and a scene between Melanie and Jackie in Sally LeRoy's (Wallace's club in *Pulp Fiction*). According to the DVD, the crew shot for two days in Sam's Hof Brau, the strip club where Ordell waits, but none of that footage was used.

Foot Notes: Bridget Fonda is the main recipient of Tarantino's lavish attention; her character is introduced and segued to mainly through her bare feet (bare but for toe rings, that is). Fonda was romantically linked at the time to Eric Stoltz, who had appeared in *Pulp Fiction*, and Tarantino likes to put his friends' girlfriends in his movies.

Nagging Questions: *Rum Punch* is among the most cleverly plotted of Elmore Leonard's many great books, and Tarantino's faithfulness to it (in spirit, anyway) leaves little room for 'Hey, what about that?' type questions. The deleted scenes answer one question, however: When did Jackie talk to Max about the scam? Biographically speaking, one also wonders about the identity of the director to whom Tarantino was on the verge of 'giving' *Rum Punch* to as a project. In an interview on the DVD Tarantino alludes to the fact that he co-wrote *Chicks Who Love Guns* with someone; did he have any other screenwriting help?

Critical Reaction: For the most part, reviewers were kind to *Jackie Brown*. Roger Ebert announced, 'This is the movie that proves Tarantino is the real thing, and not just a two-film wonder boy.' Susan Stark of the *Detroit News*, however, deemed it 'surprisingly sluggish' for a Tarantino film, however.

Jackie Brown received a 79 per cent approval rating on RottenTomatoes.com.

Release Dates: *Jackie Brown* came out on 25 December 1997 in the US, 20 March 1998 in the UK.

Box Office: With a budget of $12 million (plus probably several more million in promotional costs), *Jackie Brown* went on to make a disappointing $39 million in the US, £6.1 million in the UK, totalling $84 million worldwide.

Awards: Awards for *Jackie Brown* were not numerous. Jackson won a Best Actor award at the Berlin International Film Festival, and Pam Grier and Tarantino won plaques at the Csapnivalo Awards. Otherwise, the film garnered nine nominations, including an Oscar nod for Best Supporting Actor for Robert Forster.

The DVD: Miramax waited five years to release the *Jackie Brown* DVD, simultaneous with its revised *Pulp Fiction*. The double-platter set also included numerous supplements, such as a 'making of,' an interview with Tarantino, the complete *Chicks With Guns* video that Ordell shows Louis at the start of the film, and several deleted or extended scenes. In the UK a double-sided 'flipper' came out and disappointed everyone in 1999, with the special edition following in April 2004.

Evaluation: Upon hearing that in *Jackie Brown* Tarantino was adapting the work of another writer, his fans might have been disappointed at first. But in reality, the adaptation process here is illuminating. A comparison of the novel to the film tells us a lot about what interests Tarantino and where his mind swerves.

Numerous changes were made between the book and the

movie, yet the film still manages to remain faithful to the broad story line. For starters, in the book Jackie Burke is Caucasian (and the suit Leonard has her buy is an Isani). Tarantino also chooses to begin his story with Ordell and Louis watching *Chicks With Guns*. In the book, they are on the streets of Miami, attending a neo-Nazi rally, where gun dealer Ordell has an interest in a particular person. One major deviation from the book is the absence of a neo-Nazi subplot in the film. In the book, Melanie (who is much older) kills the neo-Nazi leader in the course of a major set piece. Another major change is that in the book, Louis works briefly for Max Cherry, whose business has been taken over by a firm he believes to have Mafia connections, part of the motivation for Max's disenchantment with being a bail bondsman after some 20 years. The book explains more carefully how the cocaine got to Melanie (the movie's Melanie is more of a pothead). A character named Cujo replicates the situation in which Beaumont puts Ordell. There is a suggestion of the use of the word 'nigger,' but Tarantino or Jackson expanded upon it, primarily because it fits in with their conception of the character. In the book, but not in the film, Max and Jackie make love, which suggests that Tarantino has the streak of bashfulness or Puritanism that you see in Welles and Kubrick.

What's fascinating is what Tarantino *doesn't* bother to tell you, what a film in general can bear to be uninformative about. Here, Mr. Walker, Ordell's mentor in Mexico, is a cipher (a little more info about him appears in the book). We don't know where Melanie came from. Max's wife from the book is MIA, and the friendship between Max and his employee Winston is implied rather than elucidated.

The theme of the book, and perhaps of Leonard's novels in general, is how men and women size each other up. The one who most accurately assesses an opponent wins. His books often focus on a kidnapping. What's unusual about *Rum Punch* is that it lacks the kidnapping aspect, though Beaumont is lured into a car trunk ('Rum Punch,' by the way, is Ordell's code name for a deal with some Columbians). Leonard has a theatrical sense of having everybody meet everyone else at some point. Melanie even meets Jackie in a club by accident (as noted previously, a scene that appears to have been shot but which is not included as a deleted scene on the disc). Leonard's characters, like Tarantino's, are adept at knowing consciously and using the social codes that Goffman suggests are mostly unconscious.

Jackie Brown was just one of four fine Elmore Leonard adaptations that appeared during a flurry of enthusiasm for the writer in the 1990s. The trend started with *Get Shorty* (1995), Barry Sonnenfeld's deft, stylish adaptation starring John Travolta (in which The Mythology indicates that Tarantino had to convince the actor to appear). That was followed by *Touch* (1997), Paul Schrader's adaptation of Leonard's more offbeat tale of a miracle healer. Following *Jackie Brown*, also in 1997, came Steven Soderbergh's career-energizing adaptation of *Out Of Sight* (1998). Common to all these movies is a love for Leonard's intricate plotting and realistic yet charging dialogue, and it is important that most of what's in the film comes from the book. (Two other novelists whose skill with chat should be investigated as influences on Tarantino's dialogue are mystery writers Charles Willeford, who wrote *Miami Blues*, and George V. Higgins, author of *The Friends Of Eddie Coyle*.)

In the end it was good for Tarantino to put his talent in the hands of a fellow artist with whom he was simpatico. With Leonard, he could honour a beloved writer yet pursue his own movie obsessions. In the end, Tarantino made one of the best Leonard adaptations and one of the best crime films of the 1990s, and one that has not aged at all. *5/5*

7. Pulp Exhaustion

He must have been tired. Or worried. Or maybe just pissed off. In any case, after the promotion of *Jackie Brown*, and one or two other tasks, Tarantino disappeared.

He appears to have receded into the depths of his new home in Hollywood Hills, where he watched a lot of movies in the screening room that he'd spent a year designing and building. He emerged only a few times.

What could have caused his sudden hermit-like behaviour? One theory is that Tarantino was disturbed by the lack of reaction to *Jackie Brown*, which not only the director but most critics thought was his most mature work. But the fact that it took so long for a DVD to come out hints at some turmoil behind the scenes.

In support of that film, Tarantino did the usual press junketry, now almost an art form in itself. Then in April 1998 he surprised everyone yet again by suddenly turning toward live theatre. Though Tarantino hadn't been in a play since his teenage years, director Leonard Foglia asked him to appear in his production of Frederick Knott's thriller *Wait Until Dark*. Tarantino played Harry Roat (the Alan Arkin role from the 1967 movie) opposite Marisa Tomei (replacing Jennifer Jason Leigh, who dropped out early in the show's production) as the blind Susy Hendrix, who is terrorized by hoods because she possesses, unknowingly, a toy stuffed with valuable drugs. The play had out-of-town tryouts in Boston, where the reviews foreshadowed the New York critics' views, and opened at the Musical Theatre on Broadway, with James Whalen and Stephen Lang in the cast, on Tarantino's birthday in March 1998. The *New York Daily News* announced, 'Turn Out The Lights On *Wait Until Dark*.' In *New York* magazine the acerbic John Simon wrote, 'The real disaster is Quentin Tarantino. This ludicrously overrated copycat director gives a non-performance to temper the ardour of his most slavish fans. The video store, where Tarantino has acquired his entire education, can teach you to become a flash-in-the-pan director but not, alas, an actor. His chief heavy, Roat, floats like a pothead and stings like a flea.' Shortly after the play opened, Tarantino reportedly threw a punch at a photographer in a restaurant, hitting the paparazzo's girlfriend instead; earlier he had an altercation with *NBK* producer Don Murphy in a Los Angeles diner.

In quotes that appeared in *Down And Dirty Pictures*, Peter Biskind's history of 1990's indie films, Tarantino complained about his treatment from the press. 'I got sick of the way journalists, especially in a profile, kill you with their adjectives,' he said. 'He "lumbered" into the room. "Gesticulating wildly." "Manic." You're getting your ass kicked by these little adjectives. After you suffer through your school years, most adults go through their lives and never have to hear or read anyone making fun of them ever again. That is officially gone out of your life. All of a sudden I was getting self-conscious about what it is that makes me me . . . Maybe I overreacted, okay. "Fuck y'all."' Tarantino's rise and fall, as my colleague Kristi Turnquist points out, mirrors that of Peter Bogdanovich, another future mentor. Tarantino knows his place in film history and is not shy about discussing it nor about talking about his own films like an excited geek. This immodesty can give him the arrogant air of a Nabokov – they are right, but you are a little irked at them saying so.

After the play closed, Tarantino went into what appears to

be a period of seclusion, interrupted only by occasional forays to the friendly fields of Austin, Texas, and a few other towns for his tutorials on under-appreciated films from his personal collection. There, he would gab about films from his personal collection of 35mm prints, the titles ranging from *Dark Of The Sun* to *The Madcap Adventures Of Mr. Toad*. In 2001, for example, Tarantino showed some 30 titles over the course of ten days, including the Italian gangster films *The Family* and *The Italian Connection*, *Saturn 3*, *Lifeforce*, *Rolling Thunder*, and *The Golden Stallion*. During this time he consented to one interview and talked about William Witney, the director of *The Golden Stallion* and an old-time B moviemaker who was a recent discovery of Tarantino's. The interview was conducted by the *New York Times'* Rick Lyman as the inaugural conversation in a series called 'Watching Movies With . . .' After that, silence.

But it appears that Tarantino wasn't inactive. He was working on, at one time or another, three scripts. One was *Inglorious Bastards*, a World War II adventure film; another was a prison break film set in the West and based on an Elmore Leonard story; and *Kill Bill*.

Kill Bill had occurred to Tarantino while working on *Pulp Fiction* with Uma Thurman. He liked that experience and saw a certain poignancy and toughness that he thought he might be able to bring out. (At the same time, Miramax bought the rights to the Modesty Blaise series in the hope that Tarantino might adapt one with Thurman.) According to The Mythology, Tarantino got about 30 pages in and then mysteriously dropped it (or maybe just turned to *Jackie Brown*). Years later, he ran into Thurman and felt re-inspired to pursue the subject matter. He would read bits of it over the phone to her; she came up with the idea of making the main character a pregnant bride.

Eventually, Tarantino decided that this would be his next

project. Then Thurman, married to Ethan Hawke at the time, became pregnant. Production plans were put into abeyance. Tarantino had been looking at numerous people to play Bill and was trying to tempt Warren Beatty into the role (George Clooney may also have been considered for the part). Beatty dropped out, and Tarantino turned to David Carradine, son of the fabled character actor John and a cult star in his own right, partially due to the television series *Kung Fu*, wherein he played Caine. Pre-production began in February 2002 and lasted ten weeks, followed by many months of shooting, lasting through much of 2002, all geared for a autumn 2003 release date. Locations included international settings such as Beijing, Hong Kong, Tokyo, and American towns such as Austin, Los Angeles, Lancaster, and Victorville in California, and St. Luke's Hospital in Pasadena, plus a small Mexican village 15 miles in from the Pacific Coast. The web site Ain't It Cool News, a Tarantino booster, gave the production lavish coverage and ecstatic reviews when *Kill Bill Vol. 1* received its world premiere in Austin. (I have a friend who theorizes that site poster Joe Hallenbeck is actually Tarantino; the name is the same as that of the main character in Tony Scott's film *The Last Boy Scout*.)

It was a pretty long script, and, at one point, after the first teaser trailers were distributed, Tarantino, in conference with Miramax chief Harvey Weinstein, chose to divide the film in two, with the second half to appear in May 2004.

Taken together, *Kill Bill* reveals a very different direction from the one that *Jackie Brown* suggested. Why did Tarantino go this route? Was he really offended by the way he was treated by the critics and decide to channel his rage into a revenge film? I might also speculate that it's possible that *Jackie Brown* was a problematic shoot (some of the actors in the cast are notoriously 'difficult'). Movies are fantasies, but making them is real life. But perhaps *Jackie Brown* ignited a deeper disturbance. The concerns in that film focus on ageing, missed (or seized) opportunities, and regrets. Either Tarantino was in an autumnal mood that led to the movie, or he fell into one while making it. *Jackie Brown* raises unavoidable and unanswerable questions about life, the kinds of poignant, disturbing emotions raised in, say, the poetry of Philip Larkin. Tarantino turned 40 in 2003. I don't think that anything as obvious as a midlife crisis occurred, but perhaps Tarantino, while making the film, found himself experiencing the same emotions that viewers felt, such as ageing, sorrow, and the intractable spectre of death.

In any case, perhaps as an antidote, a means of masking these disturbing feelings, Tarantino threw himself back into the project that represented the very kind of film he loved as a kid, before he had to deal with issues of ageing, sorrow, and despair.

Kill Bill Vol. 1 (2003), *Kill Bill Vol. 2* (2004)

Cast: Uma Thurman (The Bride, a.k.a. Beatrix Kiddo), Lucy Liu (O-Ren Ishii), Vivica A. Fox (Vernita Green), Daryl Hannah (Elle Driver), David Carradine (Bill), Michael Madsen (Budd), Julie Dreyfus (Sofie Fatale), Chiaki Kuriyama (Gogo Yubari), Sonny Chiba (Hattori Hanzo), Gordon Liu (Pai Mei, Johnny Mo), Michael Parks (Esteban Vihaio, Sheriff Earl McGraw), Michael Bowen (Buck), Kenji Oba (Bald Guy in the Sushi Shop), James Parks (Edgar McGraw), Juri Manase (Crazy 88 #6), Perla Haney-Jardine (B.B.), Chris Nelson (Tommy Plympton, The Groom), Bo Svenson (Reverend Harmony), Jeannie Epper (Mrs. Harmony), Larry Bishop (Larry Gomez), Sid Haig (Jay the Bartender), Samuel L. Jackson (Rufus), Caitlin Keats (Janeen), Helen Kim (Karen Kim), Stephanie L. Moore (Joleen).

Crew: Producers: Lawrence Bender; Associate Producers: Koko Maedar, Dede Nickerson; Assistant Producer: Kwame Parker; Executive Producers: Erica Steinberg, E. Bennett

Walsh, Bob Weinstein, Harvey Weinstein; Distributor: Miramax; Screenplay: Quentin Tarantino; Story: from characters created by Q and U; Photography: Robert Richardson; Editors: Joe D'Augustine, Sally Menke; Original Music: The RZA; Production Designers: David Wasco, Yohei Taneda; Costume Designers: Kumiko Ogawa, Catherine Marie Thomas; Sound Editor: Bob Beher; Casting Directors: Koko Maeda, Johanna Ray; Special Effects Co-ordinator: Jason Gustafson; Unusual Credits: *Vol. 1:* 'Robert Rodriguez . . . My Brother'; opening title card reads, 'The fourth film by Quentin Tarantino'; RIP Charles Bronson, Chang Cheh, Kinji Fukasaku, Lo Lieh, Shintaro Katsu, William Witney; for *Vol. 2:* another special thanks to Robert Rodriguez as 'My brother'; Running times: *Vol. 1:* 111 minutes; *Vol. 2:* 136 minutes; Ratings: UK, 18; USA, R; HK, III.

Plot: Texas, Japan, Los Angeles, Barstow. Present day. A woman awakes from a four-year coma to recall that she was shot by Bill, the father of her unborn child, on the day of her marriage to another man. Called The Bride, the woman, previously a professional assassin and now determined to track down the former associates who joined in destroying her happiness, battles O-Ren Ishii, now the head of the Japanese Yakuza; Vernita Green, an African-American knife fighter now married to a doctor; Budd, the brother of Bill; Elle Driver, the one-eyed blonde who succeeded The Bride in Bill's affections; and finally, Bill himself, who it turns out is living in Mexico with The Bride's now five-year-old daughter.

Time Banditry: The narrative components of *Kill Bill* are severely juggled, but with very good reason. Chronologically, the earliest scene in the film occurs in *Vol. 2*, when Bill takes The Bride to meet Pai Mei (though this may compete with the anime section about O-Ren, depending on how old she is). The next scene depicts The Bride learning she is pregnant. Next is the wedding slaughter, followed by her waking up, her getting the sword, and the massacre at the House of Blue Leaves. From there, she tracks down Vernita Green, and then Budd, which also leads to Elle. Finally, she faces off with Bill. The reason for this juggling of plot elements is discussed below.

Violent Moments: The film opens with a moment of extreme cruelty: a pregnant woman is shot in the head. Later she slaughters whole armies of men, cuts the limbs off a woman, stabs another women to death in front of her daughter, and finally kills Bill with the five-point palm-exploding heart technique. It is important to note that the movie, as it progresses, becomes less violent. In *Vol. 2* The Bride kills only Bill and is victimized by others.

Language: Little in the way of foul language occurs, though the word 'cunt' is used the way 'nigger' is in earlier films.

Key Quote: The Bride: 'It's mercy, compassion, and forgiveness I lack, not rationality.'

Codes Of Honour: One writer has asked why The Bride *did* kill Bill. She might have been able to live on with him, having reached parity with him through her ordeal of violence. Then little B.B. would have had a father as well as a mother. Well, the code dictated it. It is simply a given in the world of *Kill Bill* that if someone harms you, you get him back, no matter how long it takes. (This is why some viewers speculate on the likelihood of an eventual sequel with Vernita Green's daughter, Nikki, tracking down The Bride, or perhaps fighting B.B.) The 'ownership' of limbs, severed or injured, in battle is a running theme.

The Tarantino Alternate Universe: There aren't many false product placements in *Kill Bill*. The airline is called Air-O, and you do see a flash of an ad for Red Apple cigarettes. The important thing to recognize is that in interviews, Tarantino has noted that the film is part of a Tarantinian universe within the Tarantino universe, that if the characters in *Reservoir Dogs* or *Pulp Fiction* went to see a film, it would be *Kill Bill*.

The Music: The musical tones used most often for the two *Kill Bills* are pop tunes, followed by the sounds of spaghetti westerns and Asian action films. But in effect the soundtrack of *Kill Bill* is especially rich and can't be easily categorized. Tarantino draws upon all manner of pre-recorded or movie music for his tale. After the Shaw Brothers' theme and the feature attraction fanfare, the first song we hear is Nancy Sinatra's mournful performance of Sonny Bono's *Bang Bang (My Baby Shot Me Down)*. The next key musical cue we hear is the theme to the TV show *Ironside*, written by Quincy Jones (and later used in *Five Fingers Of Death*, which is presumably where Tarantino first heard it). Between these two poles all the rest of the music resides, either movie or TV theme music or a sombre pop tune. Other important cues from a rather lengthy soundtrack are *Battle Without Honor Or Humanity*, the theme from *Shin Jingi Naki Tatakai* (1974) by Kinji Fukasaku; *The Lonely Shepherd* by – of all people – Zamfir (whose pan flute music, it turns out, is very cinematic); the whistling theme from the child kidnapping suspenser *The Twisted Nerve* by Bernard Herrmann; the *Green Hornet* theme; *Death Rides A Horse* by Ennio Morricone; the theme song to *Lady Snowblood,* performed by the star Meiko Kaji; Shivaree's somber *Goodnight Moon*; the car chase music from an obscure movie called *Road To Salina*, when Elle arrives at Budd's; *A Satisfied Mind* by Johnny Cash, a song Budd likes (just as Ordell likes a Cash tune). The 5.6.7.8's play three songs, *Woo*

Hoo, Ike Turner's *I'm Blue* and their own *I Walk Like Jane Mansfield*.

Magpie Moments: If viewers found it hard to keep up with the references in *Pulp Fiction*, then they were in for an orgy of referentiality in the two *Kill Bills*. But there is a way through the thicket of impeding citations. Most of them can be grouped into three main categories: Asian horror and adventure films, spaghetti westerns, and female revenge movies. One of the first citations is from *Star Trek: The Wrath Of Khan* (1982), with the 'revenge best served cold' joke (no one knows where the original quote came from, though most people wrongly assume that it's from Shakespeare's *Titus Andronicus*). The Bride's toe wiggling comes from *The Wings Of Eagles* (1957). The Bride's yellow track suit comes from *Game Of Death* (1978). Elle Driver's mono-sightedness comes from, among other movies, *They Call Her One Eye* (1974) and *Switchblade Sisters* (1975), and her nurse disguise comes from *Dead And Buried* (1981) and *Black Sunday* (1977). Her name comes from the documentary *Full Tilt Boogie* (1997), directed by Sarah L. Driver. The sunglasses on the sheriff's dashboard come from *Gone In 60 Seconds* (1974). The two-tone backdrop section of 'Blue Leaves' comes from *Samurai Fiction* (1998), and the glass floor comes from *Tokyo Drifter* (1966). The anime sequence owes a lot to *Miller's Crossing* (1990). Buck's introductory statement to the comatose Bride comes from *Eaten Alive* (1977), where technically the character of Buck says, 'My name is Buck. I'm raring to fuck.' Cited in the movie itself in excerpts or on posters are *Shogun Assassin* (1980, with the 'House Of Blue Leaves' chapter also inspired by it), *The Golden Stallion* (1949), and *Mr. Majestyk* (1974). Bill's speech about Superman actually comes from a book, Jules Feiffer's *The Great Comic Book Heroes*. The final quotation comes in the form of a Heckle and Jeckle cartoon called *The Talking Magpies* (1946), perhaps a final in-joke on his own magpieism. There are hundreds more references in *Kill Bill*.

Biographical Shoutouts: Bill tells The Bride that she is a 'natural born killer,' a line that Tarantino first used way back in *Past Midnight*. Seth's 'rules' speech to Gloria is echoed in Buck's instructional speech. The Bride's finger on Vernita's doorbell is like Winston Wolf's on Bonnie's. The mosquito's awakening inducing sting reminds us of Vincent shooting up in *Pulp Fiction*.

Alternate Versions: Right now *Kill Bill* exists in a mess of versions. Certain elements vary from print to print. For example, supposedly not all prints have the 'Shaw Scope' introduction, and some exclude the overhead shot of the slaughtered wedding party right after the title *Chapter 3: The Blood-Spattered Bride* appears. In addition, according to IMDBPro, the two shots that usually immediately follow that overhead shot are also excluded in some prints, cutting directly to Officer McGraw arriving at the chapel and thus leading to the deletion of a few bars of a Charlie Feathers song. For the Japanese market, Tarantino prepared a more graphic version of *Vol. 1*. Among the changes are nine extra-violent moments in the *House Of Blue Leaves* segment, which is also all in colour, is a longer anime sequence, and replaces the 'Old Klingon Proverb' with a dedication to the late Kinji Fukusaku. Viewers are shown the amputation of Fatale's arm, and The Bride later takes her other arm in the car trunk. Other additions or deletions may occur when the two films are combined into one epic for theatrical or DVD release. One tweak was made in *Vol. 1* between its theatrical and DVD release: Thurman's line, 'I could see the faces of the cunts that did this to me and the dick responsible. Members all of Bill's brainchild – the Deadly Viper Assassination Squad,' is changed to, 'I could see the faces of the cunts that did this to me. And the dicks responsible. Members all of the Deadly Viper Assassination Squad.'

Foot Notes: The Bride's feet are a locus of attention throughout the film, from her trying to wiggle her toes out of a coma, to the blade she keeps hidden in a cowboy boot.

Nagging Questions: Is that Bill in the anime sequence killing O-Ren's family? Is it possible to be buried alive and crawl through six feet of dirt to freedom and oxygen? Why does Tarantino withhold The Bride's name until the end? How does The Bride explain to B.B. the disappearance of her dad? Why did the DiVAS disband? Why was The Bride attacked when she tried to quit, but Vernita is given a pass? Why does The Bride leave on her helmet when interrogating Sofie Fatale, lying in a car trunk?

Critical Reaction: Critics were ecstatic. *Vol. 1* received an 84 per cent approval rating from RottenTomatoes.com, while *Vol. 2* garnered an 86 per cent posting.

Release Dates: 10 October 2003 for *Vol. 1* in the US and the UK, with *Vol. 2* following on 16 April 2004 in the US and 23 April 2004 in the UK.

Box Office: With a combined budget of $85 million ($55 million for *Vol. 1* and $30 million for *Vol. 2*), the two *Kill Bills* went on to make $70 million and $66.1 million, respectively, in the United States, with $178.3 million worldwide for *Vol. 1* and $130.4 million for *Vol. 2*. With *Vol. 1*'s video release the film has made an additional $65 million to date.

Awards: So far, *Vol. 1* has won Saturns for Best Action/ Adventure/Thriller Film and Best Actress (Uma Thurman) from the Academy of Science Fiction, Fantasy and Horror Films; Best Editing awards to Sally Menke from the San Diego Film Critics Society Awards and the Las Vegas Film Critics Society; The Audience Award from the Catalonian International Film Festival in Sitges, Spain, along with a tie for Best Feature Film; two Empire Awards, for Best Director and Best Actress (Thurman); MTV Movie Awards for Best Villain (Lucy Liu), Best Actress (Thurman), and Best Fight (between Thurman and Chiaki Kuriyama); along with some 40 nominations. At the time of this writing, *Vol. 2* had garnered some six nominations.

The DVD: Miramax released *Kill Bill Vol. 1* on DVD in the US on 13 April, a few days before *Vol. 2* hit the screens. It had a short 'making of' featurette and an extra song from the 5.6.7.8.'s. The American DVD of *Vol. 2* came out on 10 August 2004, with a short 'making of' and a deleted scene, featuring the actor Michael Jai.

Evaluation: It shouldn't really come as a surprise that *Kill Bill* is so long. In fact, Tarantino began his career writing superlong scripts, turning *The Open Road* into a 500-page epic.

What is new, or seems new, is the emphasis on women. No female characters to speak of appeared in *Reservoir Dogs*, which gave some viewers the impression that Tarantino was a masculine director of the Peckinpah school. But this view of Tarantino was skewed by the release order of his scripts, which actually had started out with stories of women and love. But, as we have seen, women secretly rule Tarantino's worlds, from *Pulp Fiction* on.

Kill Bill perfectly blends the masculine and the feminine. There are two 'hoods, so to speak, in *Kill Bill*: mentor-hood and motherhood. Bill begins as The Bride's mentor but ends up as her nemesis. Yet he is also the father of her daughter, B.B. The Bride gets another mentor in Pai Mei, and Bill goes on to 'mentor' Elle after The Bride leaves. Mentor-hood has been a consistent theme in Tarantino's films (Elvis advises Clarence, Mr. White tutors Mr. Orange in the car in the art of managing a stick-up). If I were a Freudian, which I am not, I might guess that in a way, by helping older actors to re-energize their careers, Tarantino is 'helping' his own father, actor Tony Tarantino, but in reality Tarantino has expressed little if any public interest in the man. It's clear here that Tarantino is ambivalent about the subject, perhaps especially now that he is viewed as a mentor by so many aspiring filmmakers. Many of the actors he admired turned out to be crusty old coots who were difficult to work with.

Another running theme in the film is work. The killers of the Deadly Viper Assassination Squad may look glamorous, but in the end it's a job, one that requires gruelling training and the indulgence of a boss who sometimes 'overreacts'. Tarantino may be investing the film with the long years he spent toiling for others in fly-by-night jobs. Bill's attitude to The Bride leaving is more that of a lover than a boss, but he is in a sense 'firing' her. Peppered throughout the film are images of labour gone unappreciated, from Budd cowed by his strip club boss Larry to O-Ren punishing her underlings at a meeting to the operators of the House Of Blue Leaves, living in fear of violence and bizarre food orders. Before Bill finds her, The Bride has a job at a record store (read: video rental shop), where she has found a brief period of happiness and normalcy.

Looking back on Tarantino's films we see how many of his characters are loners. The Bride is his ultimate loner (at least at the start of the film). Tarantino's movies have often been compared to Scorsese's, but there is a key difference. Scorsese's characters are often supported by a tight group of friends, colleagues, or peers. The kids of *Mean Streets* all grew up together. There is an unstated alliance, even if it does fall apart. Tarantino's characters have friends, but betrayal of loyalty happens too frequently in his films to sustain a sense of real community. Will The Bride, after she has killed some 100 people, find a community somewhere that she can accept and that will accept her?

Now we see the ingenuity of having the first scene be the fight between The Bride and Vernita, with Nikki seeing the results. It's funny that Vernita tries to play the child card on The Bride when, chronologically, The Bride used the same card with the assassin Karen Kim, just after The Bride learned she was pregnant. In the confrontation with Vernita, The Bride thinks she has lost her child (Tarantino is excellent in this film at doing the narrative dance about what characters know versus what viewers know). Later, the whole ending sequence of the film matches the opening (hence the reordering), with The Bride's own daughter on the premises when The Bride finally kills Bill. The movie begins with the song *Bang Bang*, and links up to it all the way at the end with a bang-bang game. Thus, Tarantino inscribes an arc, with The Bride finding redemption and freedom from vengeance in the trip from Nikki to B.B.

In the end, The Bride steps out from behind her label to have a name, a name we should have know from practically the first sentence of the film, if we had been aware. If *Kill Bill* now serves as the apotheosis of Tarantino's work in juggling autobiography, obsessions, film knowledge, and fantasy, it is because he has been moving steadily from the world of male loners to the moral universe of women and loyalty. And in the end he owes it all to Beatrix Kiddo. *5/5*

8. Geek World

Tarantinoesque

If imitation is the sincerest form of flattery, how does imitating the imitator rate? In the wake of *Reservoir Dogs* and later *Pulp Fiction*, both wilfully and happily derived from the work of others, numerous Tarantino imitators – the makers of *film voir* – sprang forward.

On the one hand, these films had some of the more obvious characteristics of Tarantino's films, such as conversations about cultural trivia; on the other, they showed little understanding of deeper, more complex aspects of his films, such as narrative juggling and time transpositions.

Tarantino is quoted in an interview as saying that he wanted to inspire filmmakers to stop making bland, cookie-cutter films. For the most part, his disciples have made little more than Tarantino rip-offs, without necessarily understanding the nature of his movies.

If the blast of Scorsese's early films, or even just one of them – *Mean Streets* (1973) – could ricochet well some 20 years later into the 1990s in such films as *Laws Of Gravity* (1992), *Amongst Friends* (1993), and *Federal Hill* (1994), then the fact that the big bang of *Pulp Fiction* (1994) created a resonating red shift whose cosmic radiation became the background noise of many movies throughout the end of the 1990s should come as no surprise, given the cinema's, or at least moviemakers', attraction to crime films. Critical complaints about the 'Tarantinoesque' films rolling out of Hollywood (mostly from indie filmmakers) were commonplace in the second half of the 1990s, and even as *Pulp Fiction* was exploding, filmmakers were just hitting the screens with their *Reservoir Dogs* knockoffs.

As early as 1994, with C. M. Talkington's *Love And A .45*, Tarantino's influence was evident (although Roger Avary's superb *Killing Zoë*, also from 1994, is a special case). Talkington's film draws mostly upon the couple-on-the-run genre, from *Gun Crazy* (1949) to *Guncrazy* (1992), that reflects the two movies that Tarantino wrote but didn't direct, *True Romance* and *NBK*. *Love And A .45* was followed by *Things To Do In Denver When You're Dead* (1995), which featured Christopher Walken and Steve Buscemi, and *The Underneath* (1995), Steven Soderbergh's remake of *Criss Cross*, which, unlike most supposedly Tarantinoesque films, juggled time.

The year 1996 appears to be the *annus mirabilis* of the Tarantinoesque. That year saw the release of the Keanu Reeves vehicle, *Feeling Minnesota*, George Hickenlooper's unnerving *Persons Unknown*, the dating comedy *Swingers*, John Herzfeld's *2 Days In The Valley*, John McNaughton's intriguing *Normal Life*, the Wachowski brothers' *Bound*, the male hysteria of Abel Ferrara's *The Funeral*, Kevin Spacey's play adaptation *Albino Alligator*, and two films from Tarantino favourite Larry Bishop, *Mad Dog Time* (also known as *Trigger Happy*), which Bishop wrote, starred in, and directed, and *Underworld*, which he wrote and starred in. The European invasion began with *Trainspotting* and its descendents *Twin Town* (1997), and Guy Ritchie's, *Lock, Stock, And Two Smoking Barrels* (1998) and *Snatch* (2000). One good thing about the Tarantino influence on Ritchie is that it seems to have led to a revival of the British gangster film.

Also released in 1996 were *Bottle Rocket* and *Hard 8*, which could have been confused as Tarantino knockoffs but announced the debuts of directors with wholly different sensibilities from Tarantino's.

These films were followed by *Keys To Tulsa, 8 Heads In A Duffel Bag, City Of Industry* with Harvey Keitel, *Plump Fiction*, a satire on Tarantino and other filmmakers (Tarantino was also parodied in 1996's *Space Jam*), and *Truth Or Consequences, N.M.* (all 1997). You know that Tarantinoism has dug itself deep into the culture when *The Last Days Of Disco* (1998), an excellent film by Whit Stillman, a director as far from Tarantino's values as one can get, includes a discussion of *Bambi*, Scrooge McDuck, and *Lady And The Tramp*. *Thursday* (1998), on the other hand, had a more traditional Tarantinoesque colloquy on the relative value of Captain Kirk versus Captain Picard. *Very Bad Things* (1998) was part of the brief 'death of a stripper at a bachelor party' genre, which included *Stag* (1997), and Joe Carnahan proved to be the most dedicated follower of Tarantino's lead in *Blood, Guts, Bullets And Octane* (1998) and the later, more mature *Narc* (2002). *Knockaround Guys* (which has a great barroom speech by Vin Diesel about becoming a tough guy) was a Lawrence Bender production finished in 1999 but released in 2003. *Go* (1999) was one of the few Tarantino-influenced films with the visual verve and narrative flair of Tarantino's films. Troy Duffy's *The Boondock Saints* (1999) is often referred to as a *film voir* but really owes more to a blend of Scorsese and Guy Ritchie. *Welcome To Collinwood* (2002) was producer George Clooney's remake of *I Soliti Ignoti* (*Big Deal On Madonna Street*, 1958), as was the earlier *Palookaville* (1995).

Two films at the start of the 21st Century, *The Way Of The Gun* and *Made*, show the limitations in thinking of films solely in terms of their alleged Tarantinoesque qualities. Christopher McQuarrie wrote and won an Oscar for *The Usual Suspects* (1995), perhaps the premier post-Tarantino film, and his subsequent directorial debut, *The Way Of The Gun* (2000), was tarred with the same brush. *The Way Of The Gun*, however, is a masterpiece that is the polar opposite of Tarantino's approach. Yes, it's an ultra-violent, foul-mouthed, yet stylish *film soleil* (or sunlit *noir*), but few people saw it and critics hated it. Representative of the media's response was Roger Ebert, who called the film a 'heedlessly over-plotted post-Tarantino blood-fest.' But as McQuarrie was at pains to explain in the November 2001 *Sight And Sound*, his approach to the action thriller is actually a refutation of the easy violence and empty posing of Tarantino's disciples. As Benicio Del Toro laments in the film, today's violence poseurs 'want to be criminals more than they want to commit crime.'

The plot is much clearer than reviewers suggest. Two drifters, Parker and Longbaugh (Ryan Phillippe and Del Toro) kidnap a surrogate mother (Juliette Lewis) and ransom her to the prospective father (the venerable Scott Wilson). A criminal himself, the victim asks his enforcer, Joe Sarno (James Caan) to make things right. Naturally, things go awry for almost everyone, and connections emerge between many of the characters that are not apparent upon first viewing.

The Way Of The Gun is about quiet competence and Hemingwayesque grace under pressure. While Tarantino's characters tend to be loquacious, McQuarrie's two kidnappers, whose characters take the real names of Butch and Sundance, communicate with each other almost wordlessly. The film's real roots lie not in the work of Tarantino but in that of Sam Peckinpah, who liked nothing more than to rip the guts out of a guy with bullets under the hot sun while lamenting how standards in criminal conduct and violence were falling everywhere.

Another noteworthy *film voir* was *Made* (2001), actor and writer Jon Favreau's directorial debut and further collaboration with Vince Vaughn, with whom he starred in *Swingers*. But *Made* finds its roots in Scorsese and Cassavetes, and in Elaine

May's Cassavetes-style *Mikey And Nicky*. What is interesting about this underrated film is how Favreau undercuts, or at least does variations on, the Cassavetes approach, misleads the viewer with what seems to be a *Mikey And Nicky* template, and finally explores, so to speak, the Johnny Boy half of the friendship at the centre of Scorsese's *Mean Streets*. It's a good film. But it's not a *film voir*, despite its surface trappings of crime, talk, and betrayal.

But you can also recognize Tarantino's influence by the films he has inspired people to watch – and the actors he has inspired directors to hire. The post-Tarantino acting careers of Keitel, Travolta (as in *Face/Off*), Walken or Forster are interesting to chart. Obviously, other directors cast people Tarantino likes *because* of him.

Tarantino has been nothing if not a proselytiser for the films and filmmakers that he reveres, in and outside his movies. Thanks to Tarantino and his Rolling Thunder releasing company, Jack Hill's *Switchblade Sisters* reappeared on the screen, and Hill's career in general received attention, perhaps for the first time. Were it not for Tarantino, many of us would have blithely gone on without any knowledge of William Witney and his marvellous Roy Rogers pictures from the 1940s. Through Rolling Thunder, Tarantino once again became the store clerk thrusting upon us tapes of films we had never heard of. A recent release sponsored by Tarantino (he is credited as one of the producers) is *Hero* (2002), a time-juggling colour-coded swordplay film directed by Yimou Zhang.

Magpieism

Several issues plague discussions of Tarantino's work: language, violence, and his lifts. One might wish to ignore them, but then the critic draws the charge of insensitivity or ignorance.

Personally, I have gone back and forth on Tarantino's magpieism. Right now, in the wake of *Kill Bill*, I don't mind it at all.

The key difference between a geek and a critic is that a critic digs deep and tries to get behind the surface of things, for better or worse, while a geek is interested in his own hedonism, the thrill of discovery. A geek is expansive and associative and doesn't necessarily care what a film or a scene 'means'. It's the difference between the encyclopaedia and the scholar. A critic likes an interesting association, a nice phrase; the geek admires the *beau geste*, a pulpy story and its codes of honour taken seriously.

Tarantino rather combines those two roles. He is encyclopaedic but also interpretive. He is a human Rolodex of credits. His films are like stuffed overnight bags breaking at the seams. The Handel of filmmakers, he takes the whole of cinema as his resource. But he also provides new meanings, new interpretations of old moments by the way he recontextualizes them. In an interview, Paul Schrader, an influence on Tarantino, decried the director's magpieism with the release of *Kill Bill*. Much as I personally esteem Schrader, I find that opinion strange coming from a guy who mimicked shot for shot a sequence from *Pickpocket* for the climax of his own *American Gigolo*. And in any case, what is wrong with a guy watching *City On Fire* and thinking, 'You know, I could do a better job with that material.'

Instead of thievery, we should look to Tarantino's lifts as keys to understanding him. So he likes *The Ipcress File* and *Where Eagles Dare*. What does that tell us about him? If we look at those films again, we see how large a part role-playing adds to their stories, and that they are about complex betrayals.

In fact, 'magpieism' is now almost a genre of its own – look at the recent *Shrek 2*. DVDs are, by virtue of their gathering of information and influences, an outgrowth of magpieism.

Action movies such as Michael Mann's *Heat* are great, as sort of 'anti-Tarantino' works that eschew influence, and I'm glad they exist. But I also wouldn't want to miss Tarantino's informed, sensitive magpieism, which can so expand our film knowledge if we let it.

Sticks And Stallones: The Violence Issue

As Tarantino has said, any given American action film, such as the Stallone vehicle *Cliffhanger*, is more violent in a literal sense than one of his films.

But just as the blow job is more cinematic than cunnilingus, violence is more cinematic than conversation. Cinema is motion. The strip of 35mm film moves through the camera so that movement in the real world can be recorded. *Not* to use cinema to record motion is to misunderstand the nature of the cinema.

Like the atomic bomb, it's there; like the bomb, the temptation will always exist to use it. There can no longer be a world without the atomic bomb; there can no longer be a world without violent movies.

Sure, there is a certain beauty in films by those filmmakers who resist the natural purpose of film. I love the films of Carlos Saura, who among other things made in *Carmen* a whole movie about a dance rehearsal, and I love films such as *Thérèse*, about the saint, which was filmed entirely in bare rooms before backdrops and the mere hint of sets. And I love neo-documentaries such as *The Thin Blue Line*, with its re-enactments and staged interviews, or the talky films of Jean-Luc Godard or Louis Malle.

But these movies acquire their beauty because they go against the grain of cinema, like David Hemmings bopping against the rhythm of the music in *Blowup*. They provide the thrill of contrariness, of rebellion against form and function.

Paradoxically, that large screen in the cavernous, crowded room creates intimacy. And violence is an intimate act. If you are punching someone, or if you are pinpointing someone in the telescope of your rifle, you are as close to your victim as to a lover, trying to think like them, anticipate their moves, overcome them.

The cinema re-creates the thrill of violence because it re-creates with a certain amount of clarity the intimacy of the violent act. The fistfight is a cinematic and aesthetic institution. Kids love to see frenzied cowboys fight it out on cheap sets with loud thwacks and the sound of clopping boot heels and jangling spurs; adults love to see grown men engage in ritual bouts of feverish defence, designed to establish dominance. What is the game-turned-movie *Mortal Kombat* but a series of fistfights, embellished with kicks and tricks? If lovemaking is deemed pornographic, then the fistfight is mega-pornographic; its consequences are much more permanent, and its intimacy much more disquieting.

One crisp, clear autumn night in 1973, I was with friends in the now-defunct Round-Up Theatre in Portland, Oregon. The Round-Up was a run-down all-night cinema that showed triple bills 24 hours every day (and daily changed one of the movies, so that every three days there was an entirely new selection). We were there for *Big Jake (1975)*, *Per Qualche Dollaro In Piu (For A Few Dollars More, 1965)*, and *No Way To Treat A Lady* (1968), at that time all 'old' movies.

It was the ultimate parody of the all-night cinema. Men snored. The concessions were old and stale. Cops came through periodically sweeping flashlight beams across the sparse crowd. The bathroom was a nightmare out of a Turkish prison.

Down near the front sat a single man – they were all single men, they are nearly always single men – who cheered on John Wayne in *Big Jake*. 'Get him, Duke,' he'd cry out drunkenly as

Wayne kicked ass with brief, balletic violence. This lonely, probably homeless man, found some stale, fugitive solace in the fantasy of the competent Wayne creating quick justice. Many men enjoy watching violence, as they do pornography, in the movies. And those particular pleasures are still considered socially unacceptable.

What makes people respond to a movie? What aspects of the cinematic experience really get people going? Usually, it is only the crudest of emotions. Audiences weep like programmed robots at tear-jerking moments: Sandra Bullock revealing how lonely she is, or Meryl Streep debating whether to get out of the truck. They laugh at the jokes in *The Flintstones* even if they're not funny. They cheer when Rocky goes the distance and achieves a split decision. G. Legman, the dirty limerickist and analyser of blue humour, theorized that Americans *prefer* violence in their art and in their lives.

Thus, it is interesting to observe the audience of a violent movie when the love scene materializes. In *Desperado*, Antonio Banderas and Salma Hayek eventually get around to making love. The audience, which has been laughing, gasping, and perhaps even cheering at the elaborate, Hong Kong action film-influenced physical pyrotechnics of guns and men, bullets and angles, suddenly grows still. Are they more interested in the sex, or are they made uncomfortable with the real intimacy of this scene? Violence is intimacy without the embarrassment, free of ambiguities and disappointed hopes.

Violence can be portrayed in film in a manner that evokes the gladly somber pieties of concerned liberals. Jim Sheridan's *The Field* (1990), with Richard Harris, ends with a fistfight presented with such authenticity that one recoils from the concept of violence, as one does from the graphic images of the L.A. riots.

This is the kind of violence that women spectators often seem able to tolerate: anti-violent violence. The 'action' of

Crouching Tiger, Hidden Dragon is of the variety in which the female combatants, after kicking each other's ass for a few minutes, pause to discuss their feelings about it.

And it is true that as one watches a bad, repetitiously violent film one wonders what people are getting out of it. The rote fight scenes, the predictable reversals of fortune – it is as if the cretins in the audience will accept *anything* as long as it has the patina of aggression. The violent films that tend to be popular with some women, horror films such as *The Hand That Rocks The Cradle* that play and perhaps expiate their maternal fears, offer violence and aggression of a much more subtle and psychological nature.

There's a difference between portraying violence and creating a violent world. *The Usual Suspects* portrays a violent world. So do *The Wild Bunch* and *The Godfather*. *All* arguments are settled with violence, or at least the threat of physical prowess and superior gunmanship. *Glengarry Glen Ross* portrays a violent world, though no one is physically hurt. It is the violence of language, of words that are meant to hurt, chosen to conquer a foe, be it the boss or the mark.

Like comedy and romance, violence has its own conventions. One of them is The Stallone Imperative, the visual equivalent of Nietzsche's *'Was mich nicht umbringt, macht mich starker'* ('That which does not destroy me makes me stronger'). Villains dig their own grave when they begin to torture Stallone. He feeds off the pain, grows strong from it, until he bursts from the chains that hold him and vanquishes his enemies. Stallone realizes the fantasy of the put-upon little guy, who feels that somewhere, somehow, he will find redemption.

Violence is essentially a comic form. It is the beauty of the clever mind enacted through a body. Gene Kelly and Yun-Fat Chow are equivalent. An example: Clint Eastwood in *Joe Kidd* is walking up a stairway in a hotel to confront Robert Duvall. Duvall's lackey and enforcer, Don Stroud, is standing at the top of the stairs, starting to utter something along the lines of, 'Where do you think you're going?' Eastwood, with beautiful simplicity and cunning economy of motion, grabs Stroud by the belt buckle and yanks him forward, sending him tumbling down the stairs in mid-sentence. The scene is funny, the way Buster Keaton and Jacques Tati are funny. It is a scene to which Elmore Leonard pays comic homage in *Get Shorty*. *Joe Kidd* also happens to have been written by Leonard, and Leonard is a Tarantino favourite.

Violence in popular movies is about justice. When Steven Seagal conquers a scurvy villain, you cheer. If he does it cleverly, you laugh. But he must do it, because American cinema inhabits a cult of justice in which the laws have been devised by other movies. Yet there is something to cheer about when Seagal triumphs.

As Clarkson in his bio points out, Tarantino is adept at making people think they are seeing more violence than they are. In fact, the camera pans discreetly away from ear slicing. Instead, it is the build-up to and the hubbub around the violence that is most intense for the viewer.

But that is the problem with the geek violence aesthetic as seen in the multitude of Tarantino rip-offs: it is interested in the gross and extreme for its own sake; it is immature and cruel; it shows a geek's youthful insensitivity to human suffering, suffering they have not experienced in their own lives but that parodies genre expectations.

To say one likes this style of violent movies isn't to say that one likes violence in reality, or that one is incapable of appreciating analyses of violence as a phenomenon in intellectual films. Nor is it to say that 'violence' is a genre unto itself. Rather it is more along the lines of a technique, a comic mode, and a discipline, like writing dialogue. But all of that is ultimately neither here nor there. All that being said, I can only agree with Tarantino himself and announce that I, too, like violent films.

Future Films

Tarantino has mentioned numerous ideas for movie projects over the years. One of the first he announced in the wake of *Reservoir Dogs'* success was to be in collaboration with John Woo, in which Tarantino would write the script for Woo's American debut. The film, set around a violent kidnapping, never came to pass, reputedly because neither director nor star (Yun-Fat Chow) liked the direction the script took them.

Most recently Tarantino has talked about a 'guys on a mission' World War II film called *Inglorious Bastards*, in which names such as Michael Madsen, Adam Sandler, and Bo Svenson (also in *Kill Bill*) are nominated as cast members. Tarantino's *Dirty Dozen / Where Eagles Dare* knockoff is supposedly about American soldiers on death row who are given a reprieve in the form of one last, doom-laden mission. A 1977 Italian production also called *Inglorious Bastards* (*Quel Maledetto Treno Blindato*, with alternate titles that include *Counterfeit Commandos*, *Deadly Mission*, *G.I. Bro*, and *Hell's Heroes* and also starring Bo Svenson, along with Fred Williamson and Ian Bannen) concerns a group of American soldiers *en route* to military prison who escape in the wake of a German artillery attack. They end up volunteering for a commando mission to steal a V2 warhead held in a heavily fortified German air base for the French Underground and manage to avoid being gunned down by either the Germans or the Allies still hunting for them. The casting of Sandler in Tarantino's version, if it happens, is not surprising. Tarantino appeared as a blind deacon in Sandler's *Little Nicky*, attended Sandler's wedding, and praises the comedian; meanwhile, after *Punch-Drunk Love*, the formerly anti-Sandler critical pendulum is swinging in Sandler's direction.

Tarantino has control, through Miramax, of four Elmore Leonard books: *Killshot*, *Bandits*, *Freaky Deaky*, and *Rum Punch*.

He has also been linked to a movie about a prison break based on an Elmore Leonard western novel.

The Internet has been thriving on rumours of *The Vega Brothers*, a film that would serve as a prequel to both *Reservoir Dogs* and *Pulp Fiction*, in which Mr. Blonde would show up in Amsterdam to visit his brother Vince Vega, there running a club. Tarantino has sent mixed messages about doing such film, probably reflecting his own ambivalence, but at the time of this writing the prospect seems unlikely. But you never know – Tarantino, Michael Madsen, and John Travolta all expressed interest, and told magazines such as *Entertainment Weekly* and *Empire* that there were ways to get around certain technical problems.

Also mentioned is a concluding *Kill Bill* chapter, in which the now-young adult daughter of Vernita Green tracks down The Bride. He may do that one in 15 years – but before that, he might do an anime version of Bill's back-story, and how he came to have and deal with three mentors (Esteban Vihaio, Hattori Hanzo and Pei Mei). One writer in the *Guardian* also had Tarantino wrestling with a screenplay about his own father.

According to *Tarantino A To Zed*, Tarantino has also mentioned a Budd Boetticher biopic and a remake of the Dick Miller film *Rock All Night*. He has expressed an interest in certain franchises, such as the Bond series, indicating that he'd like to do a straight, faithful adaptation of *Casino Royale* (he told SCI FI Wire that he had actually talked to Pierce Brosnan about it), and the *Die Hard* series. He told *Entertainment Weekly* that he had an idea for a Godzilla movie. (His desire to do a *Man From U.N.C.L.E.* adaptation is apparently apocryphal.)

Tarantino once started a novel about his years at Video Archives (he finished two chapters). At an age north of 40, Tarantino could easily convert that novel into a film – it could be his *American Graffiti*.

In June 2004, Tarantino directed a single scene from Robert Rodriguez's adaptation of Frank Miller's *Sin City*. He charged one dollar, returning a favour to Rodriguez, who had composed original music for *Kill Bill* for the same fee. Tarantino worked with Clive Owen, Benicio Del Toro, and Brittany Murphy on the scene. Meanwhile, he told *Entertainment Weekly* that he would do a 'small' film first, then *Inglorious Bastards*. In any case, when the book you hold in your hands is very, very old, we will all have long known what Tarantino's next films, if any, had been. My suggestion? Tarantino could make an excellent cinematic tour, like Scorsese's, of exploitation films and his love for them (how about *Exploitation Film: Who's Really Exploited?*) derived from his Austin events.

Tarantino's Status

Borrowing a formula that critic Andrew Sarris used once in discussing John Ford, if Tarantino had made only one film, if his career ended after *Reservoir Dogs*, he would have been viewed as an intriguing one-hit wonder, like Leonard Kastle, whose *The Honeymoon Killers* exerted an influence on filmmakers as diverse as John Waters and Wes Craven.

If his career ended after two films, with *Pulp Fiction*, he would probably be the James Dean of filmmakers, revered almost as much for the films he might have made as for those he completed. Tarantino's aesthetic influence might have been even greater, as successive filmmakers mimicked him partially to keep the idea of *film voir* alive.

If his career had ended after *Jackie Brown*, he would have been viewed as an interesting eccentric, a filmmaker with a long career (six years) but little output.

Or what if he had had a different career trajectory. What if after *Reservoir Dogs*, he wrote *only* screenplays. Then he would have had a career nearer to that of Joe Eszterhas or Shane Black, a high-profile, well-paid screenwriter, but *only* a screenwriter.

Making the transition from 'just' a writer to a full-fledged movie director is difficult in American filmmaking. Screenplays are formal affairs, as difficult to compose as sestinas. In Europe they are often simple guides, if not just notes toward the idea of a film, as with Godard. But Preston Sturges, John Huston, and Billy Wilder were early avatars of the writer-to-director career trajectory. Industry insiders at the time must have thought they were nuts. Why would they want to make that transition? If they wanted power, why not strive to become producers or, better yet, executives? Wilder, for one, became a director to protect his sacred texts from the clumsy fingers of directors such as Mitchell Leisen. He was less interested in adding visual brilliance to his literary genius than in simple, bookish self-protection. One thing about Tarantino as a screenwriter turned director, unlike others in that category, is that his visual style is just as strong as his writing style. He doesn't just hear movies, he *sees* them.

To this day there is still something *outré* about being 'only' a screenwriter, despite the abundance of screenwriting magazines (*Creative Screenwriting*, *Written By*, *Script*) and guidebooks, whose profitability exists in a sphere of influences atop a vacuum of quantifiable helpfulness. Writers just aren't taken seriously – they are just taken.

Yet if a screenwriter moves through that delicate, ineffable membrane that separates the writer from the director, his life changes. Oliver Stone was one screenwriter who did it before Tarantino. As a writer he was somewhat more anonymous than Brian De Palma, Michael Cimino, or Alan Parker, for whom he wrote films. As a director he became a beacon for controversy.

But fortunately, Tarantino persisted, kept working, and

directing movies. As a director he has had only one certifiable stumble (*The Man From Hollywood*); yet his dark years of low esteem in the eyes of critics and viewers was due to his extracurricular activities – acting, talk shows, and so forth. With *Kill Bill*, as this book argues, Tarantino has weirdly redeemed himself without having made a bad feature film. He has lived up to the high expectations of his early fans, paradoxically doing so by taking to the extreme the very magpieism that irritated critics in the late 1990s.

9. Reference Materials

Selected Interviews With Or About
Quentin Tarantino

Peary, Gerald *Quentin Tarantino: Interviews*, University Press of Mississippi, 1998; This anthology gathers together several important early interviews, including important chats with Gerald Peary, Graham Fuller, Manohla Dargis, and J. Hoberman.

Duncan, Paul 'Edward Bunker: Top Dog,' *Crime Time*, issue No. 4 (undated), page 26.

Fierman, Daniel 'The Kill Zone,' *Entertainment Weekly*, 3 October 2003, page 24.

Pavlus, John 'A Bride Vows Revenge,' *American Cinematographer*, October 2003, page 34; An important interview with *Kill Bill* D.P. John Robert Richardson, with diary entries.

MacFarquhar, Larissa 'The Movie Lover,' *The New Yorker*, 20 October 2003, page 146.

Olsen, Mark 'Turning On A Dime,' *Sight And Sound*, October 2003, page 12.

Kaye Schilling, Mary 'The Second Coming,' *Entertainment Weekly*, 16 August 2004, page 26.

Rich, B. Ruby 'Day Of The Woman,' *Sight And Sound*, June 2004, page 24.

Martin, Michael 'Princess Bride,' *Arena*, November 2003, page 118.

Wright, Evan 'Quentin's Kung Fu Grip,' *Rolling Stone*, 30 October 2003, page 42.

Hedegaard, Erik 'A Magnificent Obsession,' *Rolling Stone*, 29 April 2004, page 40.

Books About Quentin Tarantino

Bernard, Jami *Quentin Tarantino: The Man And His Movies*, HarperPerrenial, 1995; The first of the 'insta'-bios of Tarantino, this one written by the movie reviewer for the *New York Daily News*.

Dawson, Jeff *Quentin Tarantino: The Cinema Of Cool*, Applause, 1995; A writer for *Empire* summarizes Tarantino's life.

Clarkson, Wensley *Quentin Tarantino: Shooting From The Hip*, Overlook, 1995; This author had special access to Tarantino's family.

Woods, Paul A. *King Pulp: The Wild World Of Quentin Tarantino*, Thunder's Mouth Press, 1996; An enthusiastic biography with good plot summaries.

Barnes, Alan and Hearn, Marcus *Tarantino A To Zed: The Films Of Quentin Tarantino*, B. T. Batsford Ltd., 1999; The second edition of an encyclopaedia covering the characters in, the plots of, and the production histories of Tarantino's films. The first edition came out in 1996 and went up through *From Dusk Till Dawn*. This second edition adds coverage of *Jackie Brown* and Tarantino's career until about 1998.

Woods, Paul A. *Quentin Tarantino: The Film Geek Files*, Plexus, 2000; An excellent anthology of journalism and criticism about the director.

Polan, Dana *Pulp Fiction: BFI Modern Classics*, BFI Publishing, 2000

Articles About Quentin Tarantino

Lyons, Donald 'Scumbags,' *Film Comment*, November–December 1992, pages 6, 8.

Tarantino Screenplays In Print

Tarantino, Quentin *Reservoir Dogs And True Romance*, Grove Press Books, 1995

Tarantino, Quentin *Pulp Fiction*, Miramax Books/Hyperion, 1994

Anders, Allison; Rockwell, Alexandre; Rodriguez, Robert; Tarantino, Quentin *Four Rooms*, Miramax Books/Hyperion, 1995

Tarantino, Quentin *From Dusk Till Dawn*, Miramax Books/Hyperion, 1995

Tarantino, Quentin *True Romance*, Grove Press Books, 1995

Tarantino, Quentin *Natural Born Killers*, Grove Press Books, 1995

Tarantino, Quentin *Jackie Brown*, Miramax Books/Hyperion, 1997

Tarantino On The Web

Kill Bill Vols. 1 And 2 together at the Cannes Film Festival:
http://www.empireonline.co.uk/site/features/special/kill-bill/default.asp#kil

An essay on the Tarantinoesque in connection with *The Way Of The Gun*:
http://66.102.7.104/search?q=cache:q7aIGpxatBUJ:www.flipsidemovies.com/wayofthegun.html+Tarantinoesque&hl=en&start=3

The history of the Wilhelm Scream, which is sometimes said to be heard in Tarantino's movies: http://cgi.theforce.net/theforce/tfn.cgi?storyID=5312

Information about *Pulp Fiction*'s relationship to *Curdled*:
http://www.eeggs.com/items/3682.html
The proper chronology of *Pulp Fiction*:
http://www.godamongdirectors.com/tarantino/faq/sequence
.html
From Dusk Till Dawn - Curdled references:
http://www.eeggs.com/items/3682.html

Other References

McCarty, John and Kelleher, Brian *Alfred Hitchcock Presents: An Illustrated Guide To The Ten-Year Television Career Of The Master Of Suspense*, St. Martin's Press, 1984; Summarizes the shows in the television series.

Sato, Kanzan *The Japanese Sword,* Kodansha, 1983; An English translation of a Japanese book originally published in 1966.

Kapp, Leon & Hiroko and Yoshihara, Yoshindo *The Craft Of The Japanese Sword,* Kodansha, 1987; Another detailed survey of Japanese sword making and history.

Witney, William *In A Door, Into A Fight, Out A Door, Into A Chase,* McFarland, 1996; The autobiography of one of Tarantino's favourite directors, this is only the first half of a projected two-book series. Sadly, Witney died before completing volume two. What is especially remarkable about Witney's memoir is that he actually seems to have written it himself.

Hamsher, Jane *Killer Instinct: How Two Young Producers Took On Hollywood And Made The Most Controversial Film Of The Decade,* Broadway Books, 1997; Tarantino figures prominently in this production history of *Natural Born Killers* by one of its first two producers.

Andrew, Geoff *Stranger Than Paradise: Maverick Film-Makers In Recent American Cinema,* Limelight Editions, 1999; A reprint of the Prion publishers edition of 1998, an excellent survey of the new Hollywood 'indie' directors.

Biskind, Peter *Down And Dirty Pictures: Miramax, Sundance, And The Rise Of Independent Film*, Simon and Schuster, 2004; Tarantino figures significantly in this controversial history of Miramax, the Sundance Festival, and independent cinema of the 1990s.

Levy, Emanuel *Cinema Of Outsiders: The Rise Of American Independent Film*, New York University Press, 1999; A broad survey, with excellent back matter, such as a year-by-year chart.

Parker, Ian 'Nyuk Nyuk Nyuk,' *The New Yorker*, 19 and 26 August 2004, page 134.

Williams, David E. 'Gone To The Dogs,' *Film Threat*, Issue No. 17, August 1994.

POCKET ESSENTIALS **FILM** STOCK TITLES

1903047005	Alfred Hitchcock NE Paul Duncan	4.99
1903047714	Ang Lee Ellen Cheshire	3.99
1903047463	Animation Mark Whitehead	4.99
1903047676	Audrey Hepburn Ellen Cheshire	3.99
1903047366	Billy Wilder Glenn Hopp	3.99
1903047587	Blaxploitation Films Mikel J Koven	3.99
1903047455	Bollywood Ashok Banker	3.99
1903047129	Brian de Palma John Ashbrook	3.99
1903047579	Bruce Lee Simon B Kenny	3.99
190404803X	Carry On Films Mark Campbell	3.99
1903047811	Clint Eastwood Michael Carlson	3.99
190304703X	Coen Brothers Cheshire/Ashbrook	3.99
1903047269	David Cronenberg John Costello	3.99
1903047064	David Lynch Le Blanc/Odell	3.99
1903047196	Doctor Who Mark Campbell	3.99
1903047633	Film Music Paul Tonks	3.99
1903047080	Film Noir Paul Duncan	3.99
1904048080	Film Studies Andrew M Butler	3.99
190304748X	Filming on a Microbudget NE Paul Hardy	4.99
190304765X	French New Wave Chris Wiegand	3.99
1903047943	George Lucas James Clarke	3.99
1904048013	German Expressionist Films Paul Cooke	3.99
1904048145	Hal Hartley Jason Wood	3.99
1904048110	Hammer Films John McCarty	3.99
1903047382	Horror Films Le Blanc/Odell	3.99
1903047102	Jackie Chan Le Blanc/Odell	3.99
1903047951	James Cameron Brian J Robb	3.99
1903047242	Jane Campion Ellen Cheshire	3.99
1903047374	John Carpenter Le Blanc/Odell	3.99
1903047250	Krzystzof Kieslowski Monika Maurer	3.99
1903047609	Laurel & Hardy Brian J Robb	3.99
1903047668	Martin Scorsese Paul Duncan	4.99
1903047595	The Marx Brothers Mark Bego	3.99
1903047846	Michael Mann Mark Steensland	3.99
1903047641	Mike Hodges Mark Adams	3.99
1903047927	Oliver Stone Michael Carlson	3.99
1903047048	Orson Welles Martin Fitzgerald	3.99
1903047560	Ridley Scott Brian Robb	3.99
1904048102	Roger Corman Mark Whitehead	3.99
1903047897	Roman Polanski Daniel Bird	3.99
1903047412	Sergio Leone Michael Carlson	3.99
1903047277	Slasher Movies Mark Whitehead	3.99
1904048072	Spike Lee Darren Arnold	3.99
1903047013	Stanley Kubrick Paul Duncan	3.99
190304782X	Steven Soderbergh Jason Wood	3.99
1903047145	Terry Gilliam John Ashbrook	3.99
1904048285	The Knights Templar Sean Martin	9.99 hb
1903047625	Tim Burton Le Blanc/Odell	4.99
190304717X	Vampire Films Le Blanc/Odell	3.99
1903047935	Vietnam War Movies Jamie Russell	3.99
1903047056	Woody Allen Martin Fitzgerald	3.99
1903047471	Writing a Screenplay John Costello	3.99